Justin Bieber: The Fever!

JUSTIN BIEBER

The Fever!

MARC SHAPIRO

ST. MARTIN'S GRIFFIN
NEW YORK

contents

This book is dedicated to . . .

My wife, Nancy, for the love and support. My daughter, Rachael, for keeping me honest. My dog, Brady, for those long walks around the 'hood. My agent, Lori Perkins, for yet another job well done. Marc Resnick at St. Martin's for letting me bring Justin Bieber to you. And, finally, this book is dedicated to the magic and the fantasy of being sixteen and being attracted to the face, the eyes, and the attitude of the pop life.

Introduction

It's Naptime

Justin Bieber admits to taking naps. Nap time is a daily part of his schedule and can last for hours. Now, sleeping is a rather unusual pastime for a sixteen-year-old. But then Justin Bieber is not your average teenager.

At a time when most sixteen-year-old boys are trying out for the high school football team, showing an interest in girls, and preparing for that test in fifth-period math, Justin is spending his days in the midst of a seemingly endless round of stardom and celebrity. And contrary to what you might believe, stardom is hard work. So you can't really blame him for copping a few z's.

Recording sessions, video shoots, press interviews, personal appearances, and, beginning in the summer of 2010, his first full-blown headlining concert tour—and, yes, continuing his high school education in the middle of it all—Justin Bieber's life is a whirlwind of obligations of celebrity and stardom on a worldwide stage.

And it is all happening at a lightning-fast pace.

Justin's story is not all that unusual in the history of popular music. In fact, it seems to happen with surprising regularity. Every generation seems to have their Beatles. Donny Osmond. Justin Timberlake. Usher. Bobby Sherman (ask your parents about Bobby). The formula is pretty simple. Take one pretty face, a squeaky-clean image, throw in a clear, youthful, emotional voice and soulful pop songs that appeal to both the young and young at heart, and there you have it: stardom.

But this is the kind of stardom that has been rare in recent years. A lot of recent pop music idols have come by way of *American Idol,* Disney television shows, and other programs with crossover appeal. It's packaged stardom, with no real sense of an artist paying dues, being real, or having soul. Justin does not come from that place. He was a total unknown, a nobody who came from nowhere. He had a tougher road to walk.

And Justin Bieber's success story is cut from an edgier cloth. Nobody beyond his home in Stratford, Ontario, would have known the Canadian youngster if his mother had not taped a series of very early talent show performances and put them on the Internet. Thanks to the Internet and sites like MySpace and Facebook in particular, the world knew about Justin and his talent and charisma well before record companies and managers did. But eventually word trickled down to them and the young boy and future star was discovered.

But getting discovered and getting the deal was only part of the equation. From the beginning, Justin was basically a nice, clean-cut, down-to-earth kid who, from the word go, treated his fans and fellow performers and anybody he came in contact with respectfully. Want an autograph? Just ask and Justin is happy to oblige. Stop him on the street and he is pleased to share a few words and moments with you. Justin was not a kid who was going to pull a Britney or Lindsay and self-destruct in the pages of the tabloids. He was into everything stardom and celebrity had to offer, and for all the right reasons.

"Basically, I'm just a normal kid," he told the *Toronto Sun*. "I make good grilled cheese sandwiches. I like girls. I'm good in English but bad in Chemistry."

And lest we forget, he also wears braces. They're invisible but they're braces just the same.

Even the TMZ's of the world had to alter their approach to covering him. Rather than catch him in an embarrassing moment, making some dumb comment or obscene gesture, Justin's regular appearances on tabloid TV shows have had a borderline G rating to them. Here's Justin smiling as he ducks inside his limo. Here's Justin signing autographs. And most extreme? Here's Justin being mobbed and chased down every street in the world by hordes of screaming young girls. It's reminiscent of the height of Beatlemania, and all pretty chaste.

Let's face it, when it comes to scandal, Justin is not an easy target. This is a kid who is so pure of heart that he prays backstage before every performance and is forever thankful for the good fortune that has come his way. He once hid his tutor's cell phone. One time he called a television camera man's move dumb. That's about as bad as it gets with Justin.

Justin is very much a by-product of the Twitter age. When he makes a personal appearance or there's a news story about him, he is usually right on top of it with a text message to his fans. Even if it's something as mundane as what he's going to be doing on a very long flight to Japan, he uses modern technology to bring his fans along with him. Justin has made a career out of literally taking his fans with him everywhere he goes. And he has gone a long way in a hurry.

And the final irony of ironies when it comes to Justin Bieber? If your parents are willing to admit it, they kind of like him too. Why? Because he doesn't come across as all heavy metal, punk rock, or gangsta rap. You could bring him home. You could take him to church. In the best possible way, Justin Bieber is just plain safe.

If you're looking for major conflict, controversy, and a whole lot of scandal, this book is not for you. Don't expect a laundry list of his favorite foods, favorite color, and so forth. Chances are you're already hip to all the *Tiger Beat* stuff because you are a true believer in Bieber Fever.

However, if you're up for a straightforward account of what happens when talent and luck and just being a nice kid mix . . . well, we've got your happy ending right here.

1. Crazy Town

Justin thought it was a good idea.

His debut album, *My World,* had been released November 17, 2009, and, as Thanksgiving approached, he was on the road, promoting the album with a seemingly endless round of press interviews and radio and television appearances.

However, at this point it must have all started to feel a bit mechanical and unfeeling. The normal teenage boy in him probably wanted to be out and about and hanging with real people his own age. As he munched on room service food, played video games, and stared distractedly at the TV, his thoughts were never far from what had quickly become a huge, worldwide fan base, and he thought he should do something special for them.

So when it was suggested that it might be a good idea to schedule an album-signing event at the Roosevelt Field Mall in Garden City, New York, Justin immediately said yes.

Which came as no surprise.

Justin's down-to-earth nature had been one of his most attractive traits since well before he burst onto the pop music scene. He had always put other people's feelings before his own and was quick to go out of his way to help them. In other words, he was just an unbelievably good kid.

And it was an attitude that had remained intact even as his popularity rose. The endless rounds of promotion and personal appearances leading up to the release of *My World* would have been tiring for most adult performers. But Justin's response to it all was to smile and say, "What else do you want me to do?"

Yes, there had been some wild scenes already. Hero-worshipping young girls screaming their lungs out, crying, and doing everything possible to get close to their hero. But so far, the scenes had been fairly manageable. Since Justin's security team was first-rate, professional, and always on high alert when the crowds were predicted to be large, everybody connected to the young singer felt this appearance would be okay.

Word quickly spread through press and Internet announcements that Justin would be at the mall on November 21; he might do a live performance but he would most certainly sign copies of his new album. Members of his full-time security team smiled a tight smile when this appearance was announced. On the surface, it was just another appearance by the latest big thing in show business. But they knew better. They had been around Justin long enough to know what was coming.

His arrival at the mall was set for 4 PM. But literally thousands of fans began to stake out the location hours beforehand. By 6 AM on the morning of the 21st, children, as well as a smattering of parents whose looks said they would rather be anywhere but there, were spotted in groups around the mall. There was evidence in their bleary eyes, messy hair, and rumpled clothes that many had actually spent the night in an effort to be at the front of the line to meet Justin.

Parents and adults in and around the scene were not quite sure what to think. It seemed like good, clean harmless fun. They had had their Beatles and Donny Osmond. It would probably be more of that. But the little girls saw it as a challenge, a quest. You had to be fourteen to understand the importance of what Justin Bieber meant to them.

The mall had been alerted to the crowd that might show up. Security was in place. An area on the mall's second level, well away from the stores, had been roped off for the event. Back in his hotel room, Justin beamed as he heard reports of the estimated 3,000 people already there for his appearance. It was going to be a blast.

The crowd, up till then, had been well-behaved. It was reported later that day that as many as 10,000 fans were actually crowding into the mall. Now they were getting restless but still not out of control. However, that changed around 2 PM . . .

Things suddenly became chaotic.

People began pushing and shoving. They began to stampede toward the roped-off area where Justin was due to arrive. They were screaming Justin's name and waving handmade signs. Several people were knocked to the floor and stepped on. The looks on the faces of the security guards revealed they were not as confident as they had been a few hours earlier.

Just when things could not get any worse, somebody yelled out that they had seen Justin in a nearby mall store, which was not true. The young star was still miles away. But that was all it took to incite the crowd, which was now a mob. They clogged stairwells leading up to the second level. A wave of bodies pushed through the ropes and began to press against the metal railings. Suddenly there was the very real concern that the weight of the bodies would snap the railing and send hundreds of children crashing to the floor below.

A call went out for reinforcements.

By the time more than thirty-five units of the Nassau

County and Garden City Police Departments were called in, a full-scale riot was on. Justin recalled in an interview with *J-14* magazine what happened next.

"It was so crazy that I couldn't even get in the building. I wanted to go see my fans. But I was told that if I showed up my mother and I would be arrested."

Back inside the Roosevelt Field Mall, police were doing their best to stop the out-of-control crowd. A reported five people were injured and taken to area hospitals. During the stand-off, Island Records' senior vice president James A. Roppo was arrested for allegedly interfering with the police in their crowd-control efforts by refusing to send a Twitter message to inform fans that the event had been cancelled. Justin's manager, Scott Braun, was also cited for the same offense.

Justin began to feel guilty as news of the riot began to come in. He was particularly troubled by the fact that people were injured. Afterward, he sent a Twitter message to all his fans, apologizing for what had happened and promising that he would make it up to them.

His concern for his fans in this chaotic situation was representative of his attitude. From the moment he began his journey to the top, he always made a point of acknowledging his fans' support and expressing interest in their welfare. This attitude was evident now, when he found himself involved in something that got out of control. And "out of control" was quickly becoming an intregal part of Justin's rise to stardom.

Three days later, Justin appeared on a local television show to explain his version of what had happened. He smiled a sheepish grin and said, "It was crazy and a bit unfair to the fans. It's Biebermania. What can I say?"

2. Born and Raised

Stratford is one of countless medium-sized towns that dot the Canadian landscape. Located on the banks of the Avon River in the southern portion of Ontario, the town's 30,000-plus population is involved in many things. They have a solid midlevel hockey program and critically acclaimed music and theater programs. Their education system is sound and their crime rate is low. Stratford is a good place to live.

Pattie Mallette grew up in Stratford. She was a bright, inquisitive, highly creative child who by the time she reached the age of seventeen had already set her mind on a career as an actress and singer. She was headstrong and confident. Those close to her were sure that if Pattie wanted to be an actress, that's exactly what she would be.

However, her career was sidetracked by love. Jeremy Bieber was a strapping, good-looking man. It was love at first sight. In no time at all, he became Pattie's soul mate. Needless to say, a permanent relationship would not be too far behind. Pattie knew what she wanted and a life with Jeremy suddenly took precedence over a life in the arts.

Jeremy and Pattie married in 1992, and soon Pattie was pregnant with the couple's first child. These were happy times for Jeremy and Pattie and they set about building a life for themselves as they waited out the months until the arrival of their first child.

Justin Drew Bieber came into the world on March 1, 1994.

The months following Justin's birth were a joyous time. Jeremy and Pattie were attentive parents. They wanted nothing more than a loving home for themselves and for what they were confident would eventually be a large family.

But their idea of "happily ever after" was be short-lived.

The couple had married young, maybe too young. Perhaps they hadn't the maturity to handle an adult relationship. And money was always tight. Whatever the reason, the growing tension within the marriage eventually reached a point of no return and the couple separated when Justin was only ten months old, and divorced when Justin was two years old. In an interview with the Web site Miss

O & Friends, Justin looked back on his parent's divorce with maturity and candor.

"I think a lot of kids have their parents split up," he said, "and they should know that it wasn't because of anything they did."

The divorce was amicable. Justin visited his father, a construction worker in Winnipeg, on a fairly regular basis but he lived in Stratford with his mother. Pattie, who changed back to her maiden name Mallette after the breakup, had been raised a Christian and was determined that her young son would be raised the same way. With a strong support system of grandparents and family friends in his life, Justin seemed headed in the right direction.

"He was a good kid," recalled his mother in a *J-14* interview. "He had lots of energy."

The first sign that Justin might be more than just a precocious child came at the age of two when Pattie began to notice that her son seemed to like to beat on things. Pots and pans. The living room couch. Tables and chairs. And it seemed to her more than just the normal physical acting out of a baby. There was a sense of rhythm and timing to what the very young Justin was doing. At least it seemed that way to her.

That he may have inherited some musical talent was not a complete surprise. Justin's father was a fair to middling guitar player and his grandfather was said to be a very good piano player.

Justin's formal introduction to the drums came at church,

where he was allowed to play freely on the church's set. These were not the pots and pans he had gotten used to, but it quickly became evident to the congregation that the young boy had innate talent. His timing on the drum kit and the way he held the sticks was light-years ahead of where a child his age should be. And as intense as a two-year-old drummer could be while playing the instrument, that was the look members of the church saw on Justin's face. The congregation was more than willing to help Justin's musical aspirations along and would regularly bring drums over to Pattie's house so that her son could practice on the real thing.

Occasionally Justin's drumming would get annoying, but his mother could sense that this interest in music would lead him somewhere. So Pattie was tolerant.

"My mom bought me my first drum set when I was four," Justin recalled in his Miss O & Friends interview. That purchase might not have seemed like such a big deal, but the drum set was something Justin's mother could not really afford. Times were tough and Pattie would often work low-paying office jobs just to have enough money to cover the bare essentials. Pattie was a proud woman and would never consider welfare. The level of poverty that Justin and his mother experienced has long been a big part of Justin's rags-to-riches story.

In an interview with *Entertainment Weekly,* Pattie acknowledged their once-dire straits. "We were living below the poverty line," she said. "We had a roof over our heads and we had food in the house but we really struggled."

However, in a December 2009 interview with *Maclean's* magazine, Justin indicated that the whole poverty thing may have been a bit overblown.

"I wasn't poor," he recalled, contradicting his mother. "But I definitely did not have a lot of money. I couldn't afford to get a lot of new clothes a lot of the time. We could not afford to own a home. But I had a roof over my head and I grew up getting everything that I wanted."

Justin began his formal education at Downie Central Public School and later at Avon Public School. He was a good, if not spectacular, student, and according to those around him he was apparently a whiz at French. Reports on what kind of kid he was during those early years are all over the map; everything from a boy who was extremely polite to one who could not sit still, was the class clown and was always getting into trouble. He made friends easily and was heavily into sports, in particular hockey, soccer, and basketball.

And like just about everything else he tried, Justin quickly mastered golf. "I started playing when I was six," he told the *Sun,* "and after a while I started to realize that I was actually okay at it. Right now, I have a handicap of six."

Justin had an active imagination and it went far beyond the normal childhood games of army and cowboys and indians. Justin dreamed of being famous one day. For a while, he wanted to be a professional hockey player. He also went through a phase where he was captivated by the look and feel of sports cars and thought he might be a mechanic or a race car driver. Friends often reported that Justin would spend hours looking at himself in the mirror and would practice signing his autograph.

But in later years he often looked back on those childhood antics and laughed. "I was never that kid that was 'I want to be famous or I want to be out there'," he told the *Toronto Sun*. "I was just being a regular kid. I didn't think about career stuff. I did a lot of stuff but everything to me was a hobby."

He was your basic ham, seeking attention at every turn. Early home movies always found Justin striking an exaggerated pose or making a face. It was not uncommon for Justin to unexpectedly begin to break dance on city streets. This was the public Justin that family and friends knew.

There was also a private side that few people knew about.

By the time Justin reached age three, he was already showing signs of being a musical prodigy. In less than a year he had taught himself how to play the drums in a reasonably professional manner. Stunned by his emerging talents, Pattie began putting much of her meager income into an endless array of musical instruments to challenge her son, which she hoped might steer his life toward the artistic direction that had eluded her.

First up was the guitar. It was only a cheap Walmart

special, but Justin mastered it by the age of six, thanks to a whole lot of help. Justin's more musically inclined friends were more than willing to come over and teach him some very basic chords. He fondly recalled that the very first song he learned was "Smoke on the Water" by the band Deep Purple. Justin's father was also very much in his young son's life, especially when it came to his musical education. He would stop by regularly and teach Justin the guitar parts to such classic rock songs as "Knockin' on Heaven's Door" by Bob Dylan and "Give a Little Bit" by Supertramp.

Following in short order were his budding talent for both piano and trumpet.

Those in the family's inner circle were amazed that Justin had mastered so many instruments at such a young age. However, Justin, in an interview with the Web site Neon Rainbow, maintained that it was no big deal. "I was just a kid messing around and having fun. I wasn't taking any of it real seriously."

On the other hand, Justin's mother was beginning to take her son's talents very seriously. Pattie would often marvel at Justin's ability to immediately master a piece of music he was hearing for the first time. This talent became evident when Justin was five. After he heard a song on the radio he immediately ran to his keyboard and, in a matter of minutes, had figured out the notes and was playing it exactly the way he had heard it.

Pattie had been an aspiring singer at one point in her life. And because of her love of voice, there was always music in Justin's house. Pattie's taste ran to old-school R&B like Michael Jackson, Stevie Wonder, and Boyz II Men. Just about any time of the day, you could count on hearing in Justin's home the likes of "On Bended Knee," "End of the Road," "Bad," or just about anything by Tracy Chapman. Justin would absorb the music and, in particular, the different singing styles like a sponge.

By age ten, it seemed natural that Justin began to sing. Those who heard his first efforts at singing classic soul were mostly amused and somewhat impressed. He was young and on the right track. Once again, this self-taught approach to singing soon began to bear fruit. His early, raw interpretation of classic Motown soon morphed into a smoother, pop-oriented style that suited his vocal limitations perfectly.

"I was just singing," he told *Maclean's* of his early attempts. "I was never trying to be like anybody. I definitely had people that I looked up to but I never tried to sound like them."

However, there was a sense that Justin was very good for his age. Pattie and her son would watch the television talent show *American Idol* every week. And at some point during the show, Justin would always turn to his mother and say he was good enough to be on that show. Good enough but not yet old enough.

And so Justin continued to sing in the house but nowhere else.

While proud and supportive of her son's talents, Pattie's Christian values put her in the middle of some very mixed emotions when it came to where her son's developing talents might take him. On the one hand, she would have no problem with her son making a career in music. But she had long heard stories about young music stars and the vices and temptations that had ruined their lives and careers. Privately, she would have preferred that Justin keep his talents in the Church, either as a youth pastor or as a recording artist on a Christian record label. However, since it was all still a big game to Justin at that point, Pattie kept her thoughts to herself and hoped for the best.

Justin turned twelve in 2006, still very much a normal kid. You could walk down the main street of Stratford just about any day of the week and bump into Justin and his friends hanging out and, well, just being kids. Justin was a regular in nearby parks, perfecting his skateboard talents. Occasionally he would wander through Fundamentals Books & Toys but, more often than not, his final destination would be Long & McQuade music store, poring over the instruments and sometimes picking one up and playing it to the amusement of the store employees.

And like any twelve-year-old boy, Justin was starting to like girls.

He had developed his first crush on a girl around that time, had taken forever to work up the courage to ask her out, and then was devastated when she turned him down.

He remembered an occasion that ended in disaster when he accidentally spilled spaghetti on his date's shirt. He also described his first kiss at a school dance as "magical."

By all accounts, though, Justin was apparently too shy to approach girls directly and would often count on his friends to pave the way for him to make his move. But once introduced, most girls were immediately attracted to his boyish good looks and shy demeanor.

"I dated another girl for about a month," he told *Details* magazine. "It was no serious thing. But when we broke up, my stomach hurt for a couple of days and then I was over it."

His mother Pattie recalled in a *J-14* conversation that Justin could be very generous with girls he liked. "The very first big crush he had in the seventh grade, he took her to a jewelry store. He would always send flowers."

On the surface, Justin appeared to be the ideal son—respectful to his mother and family members and never in trouble with the law. Well, almost never.

One night, Pattie was awakened from sleep by a knock on the door. She opened it to find the police standing there with Justin in tow. Justin recalled what happened in a Showbizspy.com article.

"It was 3 AM. So a bunch of us sneaked out of the house to go meet some girls. But the cops stopped us and were like 'What are you boys doing out so late?'"

Before he knew it, Justin was in the backseat of a police squad car. When he got home, his mother was the angriest he had ever seen her. Justin did not protest when she grounded him for a month. He would often recall that the memory of that look on his mother's face kept him from ever getting into trouble again.

Sports and music continued to be the focal points of his life. But like nearly everything else, he did not take them seriously. Those who had come to know Justin's musical talents would occasionally comment to Pattie that her son might have a music career in his future. Pattie would good-naturedly change the subject, all the while thinking that her son might be that one in a million with the talent to make it. But that would take serious commitment. Justin was only twelve.

Nobody made a career choice or life decision at age twelve.

And so, it was in the spirit of fun and good times that one day Justin decided to enter Stratford's local talent contest, Stratford Idol. He had no expectation of winning the four-week-long elimination-style event that offered a first-place prize of studio recording time and professional recording microphones. All he was interested in was entering the contest, getting up on stage, and having a few laughs in front of an audience.

Pattie encouraged her son as the contest neared. Justin picked out a song and practiced it constantly. Pattie admired her son's dedication. But she sensed that Justin might be in over his head. Stratford Idol may have focused on local talent, but it had the reputation of being somewhat of a semi-professional show. On the day of the contest Justin discovered the reason why. Almost all the other contestants were more polished and had the luxury of having vocal coaches. Nevertheless, Justin was not concerned.

His rendition of Matchbox 20's song "3 AM" was a pure, soulful hit, made all the more entertaining by Justin's natural charisma and enthusiasm. There was nothing put on or forced about his performance. To those in attendance, Justin looked like he was simply enjoying himself. Justin's performance would earn him second prize.

"You knew there was something special about him," Stratford resident Mimi Price told the *Toronto Star*. "But we thought, give him a couple of years of voice training and he would have the whole package. He was definitely up for the challenge and he had the charisma. He just didn't have the experience."

As a result of his Stratford Idol victory, Justin was reveling in being a small-town hero. His growing awareness of his abilities was blossoming. Who could argue that Justin was quite talented? Certainly you were not going to get an argument from Justin.

Flushed with the excitement of his Stratford Idol debut, Justin impulsively decided he could do this for a living. His mother was not sure but she ultimately went along with his plan to open his guitar case in front of a local theater and sing and play for donations. That summer, when his friends would be hanging out, shooting hoops or playing golf, Justin took to the streets. Crowds gathered with regularity. They watched with amazement as Justin confidently sang up a storm, with earnest renditions of Edward McCain's "I'll Get By," Lifehouse's "You and Me," and the classic soul/gospel song that had been done by everybody, but most famously by Joe Cocker, "Cry Me a River." Given his notoriety from the Stratford Idol show, it was no surprise that he received a big response for his version of "3 AM."

Buskers on Canadian streets are fairly common and the response is usually polite applause and maybe a few coins tossed into a guitar case. But those who happened down the street where Justin was playing were stopped dead in their tracks by his performances. Even as a young child, his playing and singing were flawless and assured. Yes, he was untrained and there were occasional gaffs in his vocal delivery. But nobody came away from those early street-corner gigs thinking that he did not have quite a bit of talent and considerable potential. They responded by throwing many coins and a lot of bills into his guitar case.

Eldon Gammon, the house manager of the Avon Theater, had a front-row seat for Justin's sidewalk performances. Gammon laughingly related to the *Toronto Star* that Justin was "the little guy with the big voice."

Gammon continued: "It almost seemed like the guitar was bigger than he was. Student groups [that were there for a theater performance] poured around him. The five-minute call [for audience members to enter the theater] and we would have to drag them away from him. He had a good persona with people. He was always very polite. He always said thank you."

Justin would earn an average of Can$200 a day for his efforts—almost Can$3,000 total for his first-ever public performances. The family could have used the money for more important things. But true to his generous nature, Justin used the money to take his mother on the first vacation they ever had.

They went to Disneyland.

3. THE HUNT FOR JUSTIN BIEBER

The theater where Justin had his first brush with stardom was relatively small and had limited seating. Consequently, when Justin sent sparks flying with his performance of "3 AM," a lot of his family and friends did not see it.

That is when, in the spirit of sharing, Justin and his mother entered the YouTube age.

Pattie knew enough about the new technology that she decided to post the video of her son's Stratford Idol performance and send family members the link to it. Justin has acknowledged, "I just did that for my family and friends," and that he was not expecting anything more to come of it.

That early performance video had the desired result. Justin's relatives loved the clip of him singing and, as all polite family members do, told Pattie and Justin that he was quite good. Mission accomplished? Well, not quite. Because, as Pattie and Justin would soon find out, putting something on the Internet can open it up to the world.

If you happened to be surfing the Internet at that time, came across the handle "kidrauchi," and clicked on it out of curiosity, then you would have seen Justin singing on camera for the very first time. And you would have come away from the viewing thinking that the young boy was actually pretty good, by amateur standards. And then promptly forgotten about it.

But as these things often happen, the family members who saw that initial clip thought so much of the performance that they passed the link on to their friends, who, in turn, passed it on to their friends. In the best sense of the word, the dominos had begun to fall. Justin and his mother soon began getting feedback from complete strangers who had stumbled upon the video.

Pattie's initial reaction was concern that complete strangers were watching her son on the Internet because she had heard the stories about cyber-stalkers. But as time passed, she became more comfortable with YouTube and, with Justin's insistence that it was harmless, they decided to make and post another video.

Those first videos were very low-tech in nature, shot in places like Justin's bedroom or some other part of the house, with Pattie handling the camera and fighting to avoid a shaky image. Justin sang as only a twelve-year-old could, performing songs by favorite artists such as Stevie Wonder, Michael Jackson, and Boyz II Men. For him, it was just a lot of fun.

"At first I didn't know if this is what I wanted," he told TheStar.com. "But I really did love the spotlight and being the center of attention."

But as the days and weeks went by and the handful of people who were tuning in to see Justin's latest YouTube performance grew to hundreds and then thousands, interest in Justin began to slowly but surely grow. In an era when even YouTube and Facebook videos seem to have a professional look to them, Justin's simply edited, unpretentious performance clips, often shot against such backdrops as a wall of sports and pop star posters, were winning over even the most jaded Internet viewers. Pattie was astonished to find that her son had become an online sensation.

But while thousands of people were checking out Justin's videos, his closest friends didn't have a clue, and, according to Justin, all the secrecy was by design.

"I didn't tell my friends because they didn't really know that I could sing," he told *Billboard*. "They knew me for playing sports. I just wanted to be a regular kid and I knew they wouldn't treat me the same way if I told them."

This desire to fly under the radar was consistent with Justin's personality. Yes, he would take every opportunity to be the center of attention, but there was always a line he would not cross. Whether he was afraid of ridicule or, even worse, jealousy, Justin always seemed to sense when it was time to pull back.

Justin's mushrooming Internet popularity eventually came to the attention of Toronto-based Rapid Discovery Media, a company that helped get videos of aspiring performers the maximum amount of exposure on the Internet. Pattie and Justin were still not quite sure what to make of all this interest but agreed to allow the company to help produce and edit the videos on a more polished level and to promote them to the largest possible pool of viewers.

With Rapid Discovery Media's help, professionally rendered videos began to appear with regularity. Justin was warming to the idea of being an Internet star and, with a series of new clips of the youngster singing songs by Usher, Justin Timberlake, Stevie Wonder, and Aretha Franklin, it became obvious to viewers that he was maturing as a performer.

His voice, now a youthful mixture of pop and rhythm-and-blues influences, was smooth, emotional, and, above all, believable. He was no longer a kid playing at being a rock star; now he was a kid with some very professional instincts. And although the low-tech nature of the videos did not allow him to fully develop his stage presence, one could see that Justin was quite assured in front of the camera and would almost certainly feel at home in front of an audience of thousands.

An indication that Justin's video presence was spreading came not long after the video of him singing Chris Brown's "With You" was posted. One day the phone rang and it was Chris Brown on the other end of the line. Justin's jaw dropped.

During their brief conversation, the platinum-selling superstar praised Justin's version of the song and encouraged him. He told Justin to keep it up, and that a lot of people, including real live superstars, appreciated what he was doing. If ever there was a sign about which path Justin's life should take, Brown's phone call was it. He was on cloud nine for days following the call.

Justin's clips were now being seen all over the world. E-mails and good wishes were coming in from everywhere and the number of hits on Justin's clips topped a million. With the increase in viewership came the inevitable offers from people who wanted to help Justin professionally.

Or as Pattie would often think in those early days, to take advantage of him.

At one point, Pattie was contacted by talk-show host Maury Povich, who invited Justin to appear on a segment of his nationally syndicated television program. Pattie's Christian beliefs were immediately put to the test. Pattie knew that Povich's show was notorious for its shocking and very adult and explicit subject matter that often made its guests targets of humiliation. It did not take long for her to realize that she wanted no part of trash television for her son and politely turned the offer down.

Similarly, a seemingly endless number of managers and agents promised Pattie and Justin instant stardom, hit records, and a whole lot of money if they would only sign a contract with them. To Justin this sounded unbelievable. To Pattie it all sounded too good to be true.

Justin recalled in a *Maclean's* interview that his mother was quick to say no to all of the offers.

"My mom was basically like, 'Justin, I don't think this is going to happen. It's not going to work. We don't have a lawyer and we don't have any money for a lawyer. We're not going to just sign something that we don't know what it is.'"

Justin liked the attention and, being a kid, he was pretty much ready to jump right in. But he realized his mother knew what was best for him and so he let the offers and attention slide by and went to hang out with his friends.

At age twenty-eight, Scott "Scooter" Braun was a veteran of the hip-hop music scene. He had made Atlanta his home base and had risen through the ranks as a promoter and marketer while rubbing shoulders with such industry heavyweights as Usher, Ludacris, and Jermaine Dupri. A real go-getter, with a biting sense of humor but also an approach that was straightforward and truthful, Braun had recently broken into management by signing teen star Asher Roth to a long-term deal. But for Braun, this was only the beginning. His goal was to discover and manage at least three new stars within the next year.

And in 2007, he was working hard to make that happen.

One day Braun was on the Internet, checking out the videos of a prospective client. He was watching a singer performing Aretha Franklin's "Respect." In a *Billboard* magazine interview, Braun described what happened next: "There was a related video of Justin singing the same song, and I clicked on it thinking it was the same kid I had been looking at. I watched and then realized that the kid I was now looking at was twelve years old."

In a marathon viewing session, Braun tracked down and played nearly all of Justin's clips. In the end, he knew that Justin was amazing and was somebody he wanted to represent. Now all he had to do was track him down, which was not going to be easy. But Braun recalled in an interview with TheStar.com that finding Justin immediately became an obsession. "I was blown away that a little kid had a range like that. Then I stalked him."

Braun was nothing if not persistent. He went online and searched through photo archives until he found images of Justin busking in front of the Avon Theater. From that bit of information, he was able to narrow down his search to the city of Stratford. Eventually Braun tracked down Justin's school. He then approached school board members who heard him out but were reluctant to furnish information on how to contact Justin. Stratford's response to Scott Braun's inquiries was small-town protectiveness at its finest. But Braun could not be discouraged.

"I was really impressed with how young he was and how he was holding a crowd," Braun said in a CTV-W5 interview. "He was a raw talent and my gut just went off and said 'I need to find this kid.'"

The hunt continued. Braun's sincerity began to melt away the small-town suspicions about the slick-talking stranger from a big city in the United States. He persisted in searching out Bieber family members and eventually came across an aunt who agreed to pass along his contact information to Pattie.

By the time Pattie received Braun's message, she had become fed up with dealing with supposed agents, managers, promoters, and all manner of morally suspect music people who wanted to get their hooks into her son. She considered ignoring Braun but was so frustrated at that point that she decided to call him up and listen to his pitch just to get rid of him.

Pattie contacted Braun. What she envisioned as being at most a fifteen-minute conversation turned into a two-hour talk. Braun laid out exactly how talented he thought Justin was, how he planned to market him to the world, and how he would help Justin avoid all the pitfalls that had ruined young performers' careers in the past. By the time Pattie hung up, her mother's intuition was racing.

She sensed a basic honesty and sincerity in Braun. She

also admired his straightforwardness and the fact that he appeared to have Justin's long-term interests at heart.

Justin's assessment of Braun echoed that of his mother. "It turned out that he was a cool guy."

And when Braun offered to fly Justin and Pattie to Atlanta, no strings attached, to hear him out in person, his sincerity rang true.

But being a religious woman, Pattie needed a confirmation of her feelings from a much higher authority. Pattie asked for and received a meeting with her church elders to discuss the issue. One of her lingering concerns was that her son would be thrust into a questionable pop music world rather than a Christian environment. There would be temptations that her preteen son might or might not be able to handle. She had heard the expression "sex, drugs, and rock and roll" for years and had paid it little mind. All of a sudden, she took it seriously. These were some of the things Pattie discussed with the elders. They heard her hopes and fears and deliberated. Finally they came back and told her that they felt it would be safe to take the next step and to see what Braun had to offer.

Pattie and Justin boarded a plane bound for Atlanta. It was all part of a big adventure into the unknown.

Justin had no idea what was going to happen. Not surprisingly, he was thinking like a normal thirteen-year-old. All this talk about being a big star sounded cool, as

long as it was something he could do when he wasn't
chillin' with his friends.

As the plane taxied down the runway and lifted off,
Pattie said a silent prayer that everything would turn out
all right.

4. JUSTIN WHO?

Atlanta was nothing like Stratford.

That was the first thing Justin and Pattie thought as their plane flew in low over the city. The skyscrapers that reached high into the sky. The freeways that crisscrossed in and out of Atlanta and all the outlying suburbs. This was a place where people moved fast and decisions were made at the drop of a hat. Atlanta was a metropolitan center where a lot of big things were done on a daily basis. Justin probably felt that this could become a second home.

During a lengthy meeting with Justin and Pattie, Braun was diligent, yet comforting and enthusiastic as he laid out his ideas on how Justin's career should progress. He was big on continuing to put more videos on You-Tube. But he felt that rather than spend a lot of money

and give them big-time, professional polish, future performance clips with a low-tech, intimate look and feel
would be most appealing to his audience.

During that meeting, it all seemed to make sense to
Pattie. She was particularly attuned to the notion that Braun
repeatedly drove home, that Justin's career would be long-
term and that he would be dealt with in an honest manner. Yes, she had already heard those kinds of pitches before.
However, Braun seemed sincere and Pattie prided herself
on having a sixth sense about sincerity.

Shortly afterward, Pattie and Justin signed a management deal with Braun and flew back to Stratford to get
their affairs in order and to start packing in preparation for
a temporary move to Atlanta. Those final days in Stratford
were filled with a whirlwind of emotions. By now word
had spread that Justin had signed with a big-time manager
and that he was going to be a star. Justin did his best to
downplay the situation and acknowledged that it was bit-
tersweet to leave the only home he had ever known. But
to family and friends it was already too late. In their eyes,
Justin was already gone and he was already a star.

Pattie and Justin returned to Atlanta and settled in.
Once there, they found that Braun had already been working overtime on Justin's behalf, laying the groundwork to
secure a record label deal.

Braun reasoned that the first step was to record a
brand-new series of performance clips to make an impression on the labels. In no time at all, Justin found himself

on a professional soundstage in front of a full-blown camera crew, offering up versions of songs by several of his favorite artists. Braun had suggested that it might be a good idea to do an Usher song or two, as he already had it in mind to approach the R&B superstar about being Justin's mentor. Justin did not have to be prodded in that direction. He had been an Usher fan for years, and as the camera rolled he was more than capable of doing Usher in a complimentary way, but one that was distinctly his own.

Justin's performance style jumped out of the clips. Yes, there were seasoned professionals guiding him, but they had to admit that there really was not much they could add other than technical tweaks. Because in all other areas, Justin had it down cold. By the end of those sessions, Braun was convinced that these performance videos showcased Justin at his best.

Satisfied that he had the perfect calling card, Braun set about making the rounds of some of the biggest record labels with the hope of quickly landing a lucrative deal for Justin. Unfortunately, Braun soon realized it was going to be far from easy.

As it related to pop music, the industry had gotten a bit lazy. It was not as important that a singer have talent and had paid his dues as it was for a potential pop star to come fully prepped, prepackaged, and already somewhat familiar to his target audience. The success of such prefabricated stars as Miley Cyrus and the Jonas Brothers were examples of what worked.

It did not take long for the very business-savvy Braun to realize that most labels were not willing to take a chance on a very young singer unless he already had experience in a Disney-style television show or an *American Idol*-type talent contest. It wasn't that the labels were not pleasantly surprised at the level of Justin's talent. Everybody Braun met with applauded the young man for being an outstanding singer and an overall exceptional talent. But in the same breath they would usually cite his age as a drawback, as well as the lack of backing by an established entity like Disney or Nickelodeon.

Braun came close during a meeting with Epic Records. The label had a working partnership with Nickelodeon to establish young performers with television shows and albums. The Epic representative thought enough of Justin's talents to approach Nickelodeon about the possibility of creating a show around Justin to prime the pump for his coming out. But when Nickelodeon indicated they had nothing for Justin, Epic passed.

While Braun continued to pursue a deal for his client, Justin had effectively made Atlanta his second home. Following the recording of the demo videos, he and his mother had returned to Stratford but would occasionally fly back to Atlanta for important business dealings. In the meantime, his mother kept him on the straight and narrow. Justin was continuing his schooling with the aid of a tutor. They would take days off to do a bit of sightseeing in Atlanta or for Justin to hang out and relax. He slowly began to make friends in his new home, while at the same time meeting people in the business, hanging out in recording studios, and absorbing as much as he could of the music industry lifestyle.

One day, when Justin was in Jermaine Dupri's studio while Braun took a meeting, a Range Rover pulled into the parking lot. The car door opened and out stepped Usher. Justin was beside himself with excitement at being only a few feet away from one of his music idols.

"It was kind of weird," he remembered in an MTV interview. "I'd never met a famous person before. So I ran up to him and said 'Usher! Usher! I love your songs. Can I sing you one?'"

Usher had heard this approach countless times before. The reality is that when you're famous, everybody wants to stop you on the street and sing for you in the hopes that they will be discovered. Usher was polite but dismissed Justin's attempt by saying that it was cold outside and maybe they should go inside where it was warm. Justin was a bit disappointed at the failed spontaneous audition but, not surprisingly, took the incident in stride.

In a 2010 interview with the *Los Angeles Times,* Usher remembered that incident a bit differently. "I knew Scooter [Braun] was his manager and that he was inside meeting with Jermaine. I didn't want to intrude on anything that was going on with Scooter and Jermaine and I thought it would be disrespectful of me to have Justin sing right out there in the parking lot."

In the meantime, Braun, continuing to cast his net wide, had contacted Justin Timberlake about his client. Timberlake, already a monster star in his own right and knowing full well the challenges of starting out young in the business, was always looking to expand his empire. Timberlake watched the demo tapes and could relate to them.

Having come to stardom as part of the megahit boy band *NSYNC, he knew what went into taking a very young talent and molding him into a legitimate pop music star. One look was all it took for Timberlake to understand Justin and to want to be a big part of shaping his career. Braun and Timberlake agreed that Justin would be flown out to Los Angeles to meet with Timberlake so that the singer could get an idea of Justin's personality and character. Braun was almost immediately on the phone to Justin and his mother, preparing them for a soon-to-be scheduled trip to Los Angeles.

But as they say in the music business, stuff happens.

Shortly after Timberlake expressed his enthusiastic interest in Justin, Braun had the opportunity to meet with Usher's road manager. Shop talk eventually led to Braun giving him copies of the demo tapes which, in short order, found their way into Usher's hands. Needless to say, Justin's clips left him breathless.

"His voice was magical and his personality was just so keen," recalled Usher in a *New York Times* interview. "He just knew how to be."

Usher instantly rang up Braun. The singer was more

than a bit embarrassed when he was reminded that Justin had offered to sing for him in the studio parking lot and that he had blown him off. Usher recovered and asked Braun to set up a meeting with the boy. It was at that point that Braun informed him that somebody else was interested—Justin Timberlake.

Braun suddenly found himself in the middle of a perfect storm. Not wanting to burn any bridges, he offered to fly Justin back to Atlanta for a meeting and a one-on-one audition. As excited as Justin was when he was informed that Timberlake was interested in meeting him, he literally jumped for joy when Braun said he needed to fly back to Atlanta to meet with Usher.

Although the business side of Braun was angling for the best possible deal for his client, he sensed that Usher would be a good fit for Justin. "Usher is very protective of Justin," Braun would tell TheStar.com sometime later. "He sees a lot of himself at that age and he doesn't want Justin making the same mistakes that he made."

Justin and Usher hit it off right away. Justin's enthusiasm was infectious and both had a good laugh as Usher apologized for having brushed him aside at their previous encounter. They talked about the process he would be going through as a pop singer and that there would definitely be some changes in his life. Usher spoke from experience, having gone through at an early age the same process that Justin was about to enter. An immediate trust was established between the two performers.

"It helped that I started in the business at age thirteen, which was about the same age as Justin," he said in an ABC News *Good Morning America* interview. "So I knew what pitfalls were out there and how to help him avoid them. I think the best advice I could give him was to stay humble through the whole experience."

Then it was time for Justin to sing. Usher was instantly captivated by Justin's oh-so-smooth, soulful vocals, his sense of performing presence, and that teen idol smile that nobody could refuse. "When he sang, I knew we were dealing with the real thing," he told the *Los Angeles Times*. "His voice just spoke to the kind of music I wanted to be associated with."

Usher was ready to sign him on the spot.

But Braun told Usher that he had to honor Timberlake's offer and let him meet with Justin, too. Usher understood and handled the situation as a professional. All he could do was reinforce his interest in Justin and hope for the best.

A week later, Justin flew to Los Angeles to meet another one of his idols. The meeting went pretty much the same as his meeting with Usher had gone. Timberlake fell under the spell of Justin's personality and enthusiasm. Likewise, when he sang, Timberlake saw exactly the same appeal and commercial potential that Usher had.

For Justin, the trip to Los Angeles was a whirlwind adventure. Timberlake was laid back to the point where he invited Justin to his house. Justin has often recalled how he got to meet Timberlake's girlfriend, actress Jessica Biel, and got to sit around watching college basketball with them on a very large screen.

Justin was speechless that two of the biggest stars on the planet were both interested in signing him to a deal. "It was so crazy to be in that position," he reflected in a *Life & Style Magazine* conversation. "It's a dream for everyone, so I am definitely blessed."

Over the next few days, Justin waited in anticipation as these two giants of the music world did legal and financial battle for the right to sign Justin. While most of the particulars of the offers were kept in strictest confidence and handled almost completely by lawyers and business managers, at the end of the day Usher's offer prevailed.

Justin made it plain in an interview with TheStar.com that his decision to go with Usher was purely business. "It wasn't really a personality thing. They were both great people and they were both very nice and kind."

The details of the deal were actually quite simple. Justin was signed to a production contract with Usher who, in turn, introduced the youngster to Antonio "L.A." Reid, the head production honcho of Def Jam Records, who signed Justin to the label.

In July 2008, when Justin Bieber was just 14 years old, Usher addressed a packed Los Angeles press conference to announce the signing of Justin to Def Jam Records.

"From the moment I met Justin Bieber, I recognized that he was poised to be successful," Usher told the media.

"He had a star quality that just comes along once in a lifetime. What you are seeing right now is the beginning of what it will be."

As Justin and his mother made plans to move to Atlanta permanently, the excitement was almost overwhelming. Just as overwhelming was the degree of change that was about to engulf them. Pattie and Justin were used to a much simpler way of life. Stratford was a quiet town. Atlanta was a big city. Back in Stratford, Justin went to school, hung out with his friends, and was home at an early hour to do his homework and watch TV.

What Pattie soon realized was that with a music career, her son would be dealing with many more adults and their demands. Producers, songwriters, musicians, managers, publicists, the press. The list of new people in Justin's world would be endless. Her head was spinning at the thought. To her way of thinking, the most important thing would be how Justin would react to it all. Could he possibly remain a normal boy surrounded by the glitz and glamour of show business? Would he become an arrogant diva? Or worse?

The good Christian woman in Pattie was anxious. She could have said no to all of this. But she did not. All she could do was say a silent prayer . . . hoping that she had done the right thing.

5. WATCH OUT...
HITS AHEAD

How Justin would ultimately be presented to the world would depend on a lot of things he already had. The look. The personality. Charisma both on and off stage. And yes, the fact that he could sing like nobody's business. As everybody surrounding Justin, Usher, and Def Jam celebrated the official birth of an almost assured superstar, only one element was missing.

Hit songs.

Songs that would be believable coming out of a fourteen-year-old's mouth, touch an emotional nerve with his largely preteen and teen audience (primarily young girls) and, most important from the business side of things, be so commercial that DJs would fall all over themselves to play them on the radio.

It would be a tough challenge. Radio station formats were changing almost daily. Playlists were getting shorter. It used to be that the Top 40 was really forty records. Nowadays you were lucky if a pop station, especially one that was mixing in hip-hop and soul elements, would play half that amount. Just any old song would not do. To get Justin on the airwaves would take something extra.

Usher and Def Jam's L.A. Reid were right on top of it. The ink had hardly dried on the contract when the all-star writing team of Christopher "Tricky" Stewart, Terius "The-Dream" Nash, and Kuk Harrell were brought in to craft pop and rhythm-and-blues songs for Justin. The trio had recently written songs for the more adult stars Beyoncé and Mariah Carey but Stewart indicated that writing songs for a teenage performer would not be a problem.

"It's just about making a universal-sounding record," he offered in a Billboard.com interview. "It kind of helps you write better because the lyrical content is limited and there's a lot less you can say."

Justin would not go the cover song route, which, in the past, had often been an easy first step onto the charts for a teen idol. From the start, Justin's music would be blazingly original.

The plan was to have Justin go into the studio and record a total of eight songs, the first three of which would come out on radio and Internet sites in advance of what would ultimately be an eight-song EP. Those involved in guiding Justin's career knew it would be a risky way to go. Giving away almost half an album's songs before the release of the album could easily result in less than expected sales. Or it could be the hook to make Justin's music go through the roof.

The wheels of Justin's career were now moving fast. Studio time was booked in Atlanta's famed Triangle Sound Studios.

Justin was excited and, truth be known, a bit nervous as he ventured into his first professional recording session. Under the guidance of producers/songwriters Stewart, JB, and Coron, he was patiently guided through the intricacies of pacing and voice modulation, and during the numerous takes it required to get a performance that everybody was satisfied with.

"I'm kind of a perfectionist," said Justin in looking back on those first sessions in a Neon Limelight interview. "I always like to do my best. But being that Usher was behind me, I guess there was a little bit of pressure."

However, Justin found that everyone connected with the sessions was generous with their time, walking the young boy through the process of a professional recording session and telling him what he needed to do to help move it along. It was to the producers' and engineers' credit that they talked to Justin in the same manner as they would to any novice singer. There was some humor, some straightforward instruction. But most important, they made it plain that there was no rush and that Justin could take as much time as he wanted to get it right. First and foremost, Justin had to feel comfortable and safe.

The first song to come out of the sessions was "One Time," an infectious slice of soul and pop dedicated to the time-honored tale of young love. Justin's vocals are alternately underplayed and out front for maximum emotional/ teen appeal and in certain respects offer a nod to a very young Chris Brown.

And even though he had heard Justin sing quite often, Braun was amazed by how "One Time" had emerged. "People don't hear it and think 'Oh, it's a little kid's record,'" he said in a PR Log release. "He's a young kid who sings with a lot more soul than he should."

The praise given to Justin on this maiden recording voyage was music to his ears. Still a babe in the woods when it came to his budding career, Justin was looking for honest opinions from his peers, be they good or bad. That those first critiques were good was sweet.

"One Less Lonely Girl" continued the theme of Justin as a romantic teen heartthrob, a spirited mid-tempo ballad that instantly called to mind memories of what had made both Chris Brown and Beyoncé stars. The song, cowritten and produced by Usher, showcased Justin's ability to be tender and emotionally expressive.

It was the first time that Usher and Justin were dealing with each other in the studio, and Justin was anxious to please. Usher combined simple instruction and low-key encouragement as he navigated the young man through the song.

In describing the song, Justin told MTV, "I think it's very important that these girls have something."

After what many felt were the "safe" choices of "One Time" and "One Less Lonely Girl," Justin broke out of the box with "Love Me," a very upbeat, clublike track that mixed a particularly potent synthesizer/pop backing with some definite dance and R&B elements. Ears also perked up on this song when Justin and the producers effectively sampled the chorus from "Lovefool" by The Cardigans into the mix.

"Favorite Girl" was a hybrid of sorts. A mid-tempo song, much in the vein of "One Time" and "One Less Lonely Girl," it also took a synthesizer/pop bite out of "Love Me." Justin's vocals were solid in his customary smooth soul/R&B mix. The song is notable for becoming a favorite of country/pop star Taylor Swift and led to what turned into an ongoing friendship between her and Justin.

The remaining four songs to come out of this recording session—"Down to Earth," "Bigger," "First Dance," and "Common Denominator"—all fit smoothly with the theme of puppy love and offer an innocent take on romantic relationships. These were not necessarily considered radio-friendly, commercial songs but they were in keeping with the idea of showcasing Justin's lyrical and musical diversity.

As the sessions progressed, Justin became increasingly comfortable in the studio environment and with that came a growing confidence in his singing ability. During the later stages of the sessions, Justin was not shy about offering suggestions about the lyrics and music and about how a word or stanza should be sung or emphasized for maximum effect. There was logic in his offerings that went far beyond his tender years and they were incorporated to the point where Justin was awarded cowriting credit on four of the eight songs.

His input on the *My World* sessions would also include his ability to play instruments. Much had already been said of Justin's accomplishments as a self-taught musician, and as the sessions progressed, the producers would occasionally give the singer a chance to show them what he could do. While there is no specific credit on the album, mentioning a particular song on which Justin played a tasty guitar line or a solid backbeat, those who were present say Justin's playing is definitely represented on these cuts.

Justin has often acknowledged that almost all of that first batch of songs dealt with young love and romance. But he has also been quick to offer that "Down to Earth" held particularly strong feelings for him, as the song describes the feelings of a young child whose parents have split up.

By the beginning of 2009, the entire session was ready for the Def Jam executives to listen to. Everything sounded great.

It took Def Jam production head L.A. Reid only one hearing to know that Justin, without having any other pro exposure behind him, could succeed on the strength of his music alone. Braun recalled Reid's reaction verbatim in a Billboard.com interview: "He was like 'We've got singles. We're ready.'"

It was around this time that another element of Justin's persona began to be molded: how to do interviews. On the surface, Justin's boyish good looks and innocent demeanor would seem to have made him the ideal candidate to do press. He was not shy in front of cameras and would talk easily with complete strangers. His impromptu meeting with Usher had proven that.

But there were elements of the interview package that needed to be addressed, such as being careful not to say anything negative or controversial, and to always say nice things about other people, especially the fans. And finally . . . if you're someplace to promote something, make sure you remember to promote it. Through practice sessions, Justin quickly figured out the particulars of the interview process and it was to his credit that he was able to play the promotion game without losing his boyish charm.

The Internet release of "One Time" in April 2009, as both a single and a video, was perfectly timed for maximum exposure on a number of fronts. The song was made available to radio stations in early May but, despite largely favorable reviews, it was slow to pick up steam. All that changed when the video version began spreading across the Internet and, in particular, to YouTube, where Justin already had a subscriber base of 40 million. Driven by the YouTube exposure, "One Time" eventually caught fire and made its first appearance on the coveted *Billboard* charts, at 95. For Justin's first single, it would be a slow and steady six-month climb up the charts that would ultimately top out at 20.

Critics were falling all over themselves in praising the song. About.com said that it "had the effect of a younger Chris Brown." *Billboard* called it "a hallmark pop song that taps into the teen hip-hop aesthetic." *Entertainment Weekly* said it was "a refreshing, age-appropriate chronicle of young love."

Everybody connected with Def Jam and Justin's management team were beside themselves with excitement. They knew from experience that there were no sure bets in the music business. But all of a sudden, with the release of only one record, Justin was beginning to look like just that.

October 6, 2009, saw the release of Justin's follow-up single, "One Less Lonely Girl." It racked up 113,000 downloads on iTunes its first week of release and would ultimately peak at 16 on *Billboard*. The song would have a short stay on the national charts but would go on to have a longer life on *Billboard*'s Pop Song List.

Once again, the critics weighed in favorably. *Billboard* offered that the song "makes a strong statement for why he is the next pop/rhythm-and-blues heartthrob." *The*

New York Times described the song as "uncomplicatedly beautiful and earnest."

Again the people behind the scenes were happy. But reportedly there were some who were looking to shake things up a bit with the third single, lest Justin be perceived as a singer of limited style.

A bit of record company indecision would mark the release of "Love Me," on October 26, 2009. Originally everybody, including Justin, was under the impression that the next single would be a remix of "One Time." It was only at the last possible moment that a very surprised Justin discovered that Def Jam had changed its mind and was going with "Love Me."

Like the previous songs, "Love Me" gathered a solid iTunes buy from fans and made its *Billboard* debut at 16. But despite the positive reviews and sales, the song would fall off the national charts in a mere four weeks.

Critics were beginning to take Justin a bit more seriously with this song. Most made the obvious comparison to The Cardigans' "Lovefool" and were a bit more reserved in their comments. The *Boston Globe* said " 'Love Me' was the essential song of the set." *The Washington Post* exclaimed that the song "was a modest club track." *BBC Music* reported that "Bieber exhibits the right kind of attitude, playful and endearing."

Finally, on November 3, 2009, "Favorite Girl" raced out of the iTunes gate with solid sales and a *Billboard* debut at 26 before eventually falling off the charts. Reviews of the single were sparse; MTV pretty much summed up the impression it made by calling the song "a funky, groovy swaggerific jam."

But while the chart stays seemed to decline with each successive single, Justin's record company and management were extremely pleased with the fact that the songs had also charted quite well in Canada and other parts of the world. This was particularly gratifying for Def Jam because while U.S. chart success was great, international acceptance was ultimately the pathway to a long career.

Justin would get regular updates on how each song was doing. He had become a quick study when it came to the business side of music and while he didn't always understand the lingo and the jargon, he knew enough to understand that his records were doing well. The messages usually caught up with him on a plane, in a hotel room, or in a car or van on the way to somewhere or something. Because, as Justin was now finding out, hitting the road to endlessly promote himself and to be seen was a big part of being a pop star.

And by the time "One Girl" had hit the charts, Justin was already on the road for what would be an eight-month odyssey.

6. LIGHTS! Camera! JUSTIN!

Almost from the moment Def Jam gave a thumbs up to Justin's first batch of songs, they began to formulate ways to market them. Given Justin's previous exposure on the Internet, including Facebook, YouTube, and iTunes, they had a head start. Justin had already laid a solid groundwork with his fan-friendly nature and that, according to an interview Braun gave in *The Observer,* was the way the process would continue.

"We'll give it to the kids, let them do the work, so that they'll feel like it's theirs."

Ryan Good, hired early on to be Justin's style coach, echoed those sentiments in the same *Observer* piece. "His fans have a vested interest in him because they saw him before the [professional] music videos and the glitz. To them, he was just a singer in a house."

However, at the end of the day they still needed a music video on which to focus their promotion and gather those all important hits on outlets like YouTube.

With the selection of "One Time" as Justin's first single, Def Jam immediately decided on a budget for a video and started hiring people who could create it. First off they needed a director. At first glance, Vashtie Kola would seem like an unusual choice. She had never directed a music video before but was already a veteran of video production, having written a number of treatments for music videos for such artists as Common. Mix in her background in fashion design and party planning, and both Usher and L.A. Reid were confident that she had the right visual attitude for the job.

The story line would be simple, as befitting the style of the song. Justin and his real-life friend Ryan Butler would be hanging out at Usher's house playing video games. Usher has to leave for a while and asks Justin if he will watch the house while he is gone. Justin and Ryan take the opportunity to throw a house party. As the story and the song play out, Justin pursues a girl he sees across the room. It's shaping up to be a happy ending until the mystery girl gives Justin a peck on the cheek and then disappears. Adding insult to injury, Usher shows up and Justin is busted.

Having Usher, already a veteran of countless music videos, and Ryan, who had several commercials to his credit, in the video helped ease Justin into a comfort zone for the shoot. They knew about hitting their marks and how to stand for the most effective blocking of camera shots. Justin soaked up the info fairly easily and came across in his scenes as if he had been making music videos all his life.

The process was much more sophisticated than the simple YouTube videos that had propelled Justin into the limelight. But the endless takes required to effectively sync the song to the story did not faze him. Vashtie ran a loose but professional set. She and Justin had developed an immediate rapport. She could sense the raw talent in the boy and was bent on using all her visual tricks to coax it out of him. There was no tension and a lot of laughs, which ultimately resulted in the footage being shot in record time.

Editing would take care of the rest, and what emerged was a polished yet straightforward video about puppy love and the age-old story of "while the cat's away the mice shall play" that truly reflected the tone of the song. Justin described the process by which he had gone from primitive webcam videos to a professional shoot as "cool."

The "One Time" video was released to YouTube on June 13, 2009. In short order, it racked up more than 2 million views and would total more than 100 million by January 2010.

When it came time to create a video concept for Justin's second single, "One Less Lonely Girl," the brain trust at Def Jam looked to slightly modify the story idea. Whereas "One Time" had a slightly hip and urban take on young love, "One Less Lonely Girl" seemed more like an old-fashioned tale of young love.

A story was fashioned in which Justin sees a girl at the local laundromat. He returns another day and there she is again. As she gets ready to leave, she drops a scarf. Justin picks it up. When the girl comes back for it, she finds a note saying that he has the scarf and telling her where to go in town to find it. So begins a treasure hunt through small town USA in which the girl finds pictures of Justin in romantic poses, with puppies, buying her chocolates, and so on, and notes telling her what they would do on a date. As the story and the song plays out, the girl finally meets up with Justin and they live happily ever after.

Def Jam liked the idea and cast about for a director well-known for putting an old-fashioned spin on things. They came up with Roman White, a veteran who knew his way around young pop stars and, most recently, had done the video for Taylor Swift's "You Belong With Me." Wanting authenticity for the video's location, White decided on the small town of Watertown, Tennessee, and the cast and crew hit the road.

In comparison to "One Time," this shoot was much more relaxed. The less-hectic lifestyle and middle-America vibe of Watertown appealed to Justin. He loved filming at the various outdoor locations. The easygoing nature of the shoot was infectious for everybody—so much so that

Justin's mother was persuaded to step out from behind the scenes and appear in a cameo during the flower stand sequence.

With one pro-level video now under his belt, Justin was precise in his movements in front of the camera, receptive to the director's instructions, and, most important, came across as sincere and believable in this small town fairy tale. He found the atmosphere appealing and acknowledged that as small as Watertown was, it was big in comparison to his hometown of Stratford.

The people at Def Jam were thrilled with the video and with Justin's maturity and ease in front of the camera. The videos promised to be an important part of bringing Justin to his fans.

Because there would be more to come.

7. STAR-SPANGLED ROAD STORIES

There were basically two rules when Justin went on his first promotion tour. One was that he had to have one day off a week to unwind—to not do anything business related. The second was that, with the aid of a tutor who traveled with him, he had to continue his schooling.

The tour was shaping up as a test for Justin on a number of fronts. Could he deal with the countless hours of boredom as well as the moments when he was playing pop star? Would he function as a professional or occasionally revert to being a teenager at an inappropriate moment? And from a purely entertainment point of view, how would he perform when singing for the first time in front of crowds that could easily number in the thousands?

Given the possible challenges and pitfalls, it did not

come as too much of a surprise that Braun, Usher, and L.A. Reid put together a professional posse. A tutor named Jenny was hired based on her experience, patience, and willingness to not let professional obligations and distractions get in the way of providing Justin with as good an education as possible. Road manager Ryan Good was on board to both manage his daily schedule as well as help mold Justin's style of dress, swagger, and attitude when dealing with fans, the press, and celebrity talk-show hosts.

"Yeah, that's right," chuckled Justin in an *Ottawa Citizen* interview. "I have a swagger coach who helps me and teaches me different things to do. He has helped me with my style and just putting different pieces together."

A vocal coach was hired because speculation was that Justin would soon be reaching an age where his voice would change and Justin's manager and record company representatives wanted to make sure Justin could adjust to those changes. There was also a publicist to handle the press and the personal appearances that were being booked.

Of major importance was security and bodyguards. Head bodyguard Kenny Hamilton and others were instructed to do more than simply protect Justin from hoards of aggressive fans. They were told to get in Justin's face and give him what for at the first sign of attitude or rudeness on his part. Of course Braun would be ever present and Usher said he would make it a point of dropping in on the promotional tour from time to time.

Last but certainly not least was Pattie, who was thankful for all the help but knew that she would be a major player in keeping Justin grounded in the months ahead.

The Justin Bieber promotional tour kicked off in early May 2009 with a series of radio station visits, during which Justin schmoozed with the all-important radio personalities and played it cool when fielding calls from hysterical fans. A stopover early in the tour at the *Kidd Kraddick in the Morning* show was an indication of how quickly Justin had learned to play this game. He was believably humble and enthusiastic to the host and to fans alike. And he was never too far away from thanking the fans for their support. An extra bonus on this particular visit came as a surprise: an on-air phone call from Usher, who heaped praise on his newest star.

June 20 was set to be Justin's official "coming out" in a live concert setting, when he took to the Sandstone Amphitheater stage in Kansas City as part of radio station KMXV's annual Red, White, and Boom concert extravaganza, for a live performance of "One Time." For those in attendance, it was quickly evident how confident a performer Justin had become in a relatively short time. His vocals were spot-on as he danced across the stage to the hysterical screams of the audience. The smile never left his face. Justin had arrived in Kansas City and was suddenly a full-blown star.

And he liked the feeling.

Live, in-studio radio chats were coming quick and fast

and Justin had adjusted to doing them in a highly polished manner. Typical of his evolution as an interviewee
were the in-studio appearances at Z100 and Much Music.
He took every question seriously, even the more fan-
oriented, "What's your favorite color?" ones, and always
responded with a thoughtful and amusing answer. Again
he was quick to thank his fans and, in the process, manage to help his latest record along by mentioning it at least
a couple of times.

At this stage of his career, what happened after the appearance had settled into a bit of a routine. It seemed like
there would always be a group of young girls waiting outside to catch a glimpse of their pop star crush. If it was
a relatively small group, Justin had no problem stopping,
posing for cell phone pictures, signing autographs, or ex-
changing a few words. But as the tour progressed and the
crowds got bigger and more physical, Justin, surrounded
by security guards, would usually race to his car or van
and be driven off.

When crowds grew aggressive, Justin would occasionally express some concern. "I'm a really claustrophobic
person to begin with," he told TheStar.com. "I love being
the center of attention but it's very definitely scary when
girls are all around me and I can't go anywhere. But I guess
I've got to get used to it. But sometimes it scares me."

For Justin, the routine was soon set. He would wake up
early and have a minimum of three hours of tutoring with
Jenny. Then it was off to the latest round of appearances.

When he had free time between appearances, he would often be seen playing video games or riding around hotel hallways on his skateboard. Justin loved to hang out and one of his favorite places to hang out was the mall. However, the growing and excitable nature of his fan base now made it almost impossible for him to visit a mall except during the hours when his fans would be at school. But while he would occasionally grumble about having to be tutored ("School sucks" quickly became his trademark phrase) or get tired and grumpy at the end of a long day of professional obligations, those around him marveled at how, at the age of fifteen, he was handling the more mundane aspects of the celebrity lifestyle like a professional.

Until now, Justin's performing appearances had been limited to one or two songs. But when he hopped aboard the MTV Video Music Awards tour for its August 28 stopover at Six Flags Magic Mountain in Jackson, New Jersey, it was with the idea that he would do a four-song set. Justin was more than up for this new challenge but those around him were curious as to how he would handle a longer set with its pacing and singing challenges. They need not have worried.

For as the lights went down, the spotlight hit center stage, and the screaming and applause grew to deafening proportions, Justin strode onstage, smiled that broad Justin smile, and launched into the set. As he ran through the songs "One Time," "Never Let You Go," "Bigger," and

"One Less Lonely Girl," his vocals were strong and emotional, his stage moves polished and professional, and you could have taken the electricity of the performance and sold it by the kilowatt. Even those who might have doubted him before were now convinced. Though still just fifteen, Justin had suddenly matured into an adult performer.

It was also becoming evident that the press coverage of Justin was changing as well. The *Tiger Beat* and *Bop* fan magazine coverage made up much of it. But now such adult outlets as *Billboard* and *The Wall Street Journal* were catching their own Bieber Fever, running articles that took a more business-oriented approach to Justin's sudden rise to stardom. The gist of these and other articles was that Justin and just about everybody connected with him were going to make a lot of money and that, if his career was handled right, Justin would eventually make the transition from teen heartthrob to mainstream artist.

Justin had always been a Twitter kid even before he became a star and he was very much in that groove during the tour. It seemed as though whenever he wasn't busy he was tweeting friends, family, the occasional suprised fan, or sending out up-to-the-minute blogs on his own Web site. So it seemed like a natural thing when Justin was booked into the massive Nintendo World Store in New York City's famed Rockefeller Center for a brief meet-and-greet and a short acoustic performance.

Word spread on the Internet and among local radio stations that Justin's September 1 appearance would be limited to 300 people. But by now Bieber Fever was in full swing and New York police and city officials were more than a bit concerned when literally hundreds of young girls and, yes, their parents began camping out around the store nearly twenty-four hours before the scheduled appearance. Security sensed a much bigger crowd than anticipated would show up and so began to set up metal fences around the store in order to keep the ever swelling crowd under control.

That turned out to be a good idea. Shortly before the event was scheduled to begin, an estimated 2,000 screaming girls, armed with cell phones, were jostling with camera-wielding paparazzi to hold their position as New York's Finest stood around, hoping for the best but preparing for full-scale pandemonium. When Justin and his entourage arrived, they were ushered into the building through a side door.

Justin was amazed at the crowd assembled outside but wanted to get a better view, so he was taken up to the store's second floor. He went to the huge glass windows and looked down. An earsplitting series of screams went up as Justin was spotted. Hundreds of hands with cell phones in them were held aloft as fans struggled to get an image of Justin . . . even if it was only the back of his head. At one point, Justin acknowledged the crowd with a wave before disappearing back into the store.

Shortly before the doors were set to open an announcement was made to the crowd. Only 150 people would be allowed into the store for the event. The screaming crowd began to surge toward the door. This was pandemonium reminiscent of Beatlemania. Fortunately nobody was injured. After the performance, Justin was whisked off in a van and gone. But the memory of that day stuck with him for a long time. The scene had been crazy, but it was one that indicated that Justin was well on the road to stardom.

And it was repeating itself on a daily basis. Justin would arrive for an event and the show's host would be unprepared for the number of people who showed up. There would be screaming and hysteria. And yes, some girls would faint. But it was all good fun and it always translated into headlines.

By summer 2009, Bieber Fever had reached its apex. Surging on a wave of screaming girls, massive crowds, and, most important, a seemingly perfect series of pop music hits that were everywhere you turned, Justin's growing influence was unstoppable. Which is why it came as no surprise when MTV asked the young teen star to be a presenter for that year's Video Music Awards Show.

Justin was thrilled at the prospect of hanging out with some of his music idols and, on the night of the show, was like a kid in a candy store while he hung out backstage before the show and chatted with some of his favorite performers. Justin came across as enthusiastic and genuine;

no doubt he put to rest the feelings of many fellow performers that he was just the latest in a line of manufactured pop stars who had little if any substance or personality.

Justin was excited as he waited backstage with his copresenter, actress Miranda Cosgrove. Finally the pair were brought onstage to the frantic cheers and yells of the audience. Miranda is an accomplished actress in her own right but it was obvious who the enthusiastic response was intended for. After some good-natured banter, the pair introduced another superstar—Taylor Swift, who sang her current hit, "You Belong with Me."

Justin thought his work for the night was over. But he soon became involved in a bit of unexpected drama. Later in the show, it was announced that Swift had won the best music video award for "You Belong with Me." Suddenly an irate Kanye West leaped onto the stage, grabbed the microphone from a shocked Swift, and began a tirade against the show for not giving the best music video award to Beyoncé.

Justin, along with everybody else, was shocked at West's rude behavior. But rather than say nothing, he vigorously defended Swift in some post-show interviews. It wasn't long before word of Justin's defense got back to Swift and she contacted him. "Taylor Swift thanked me for saying that she deserved to win her award," he told *Billboard*. "She said, 'Thanks for sticking up for me, little bro,' and I was like 'Yeah, I've got your back.'"

And so the friendship between the two stars was formed.

Justin continued down the promo trail. And on some days it turned out to be a grind, pure and simple. Take for instance one day in September, when after getting up extra early in order to get his schoolwork out of the way, he made appearances at three different Tennessee radio stations. Justin knew the drill by heart at this point. The questions were pretty much the same, over and over. The excited fans would call in. Then it would be out the door, often through a large crowd of young girls, and into a van for a ride to the next appearance.

Although Justin kept up a good front and was the consummate pro, there were days when he seemed tired and bored and reverted to what he really was: a teenager. He was never supposed to be far from his bodyguards but there were occasions when Justin would leap out of his van when it returned to the hotel and go running through the hotel lobby with the guards and his mother in hot pursuit. Occasionally he would become snippy and argumentative with those around him. And true to the promise that was made before the promo tour started, there was always somebody to put him in his place, gently but firmly.

Justin had often said that it did not bother him to be constantly surrounded by adults but it was becoming increasingly obvious that he still needed to be around kids his own age and to just do kid things. At Justin's request, two lifelong friends from back in Stratford, Chaz and Ryan, were occasionally flown out to wherever Justin was, to spend the day together just hanging out. They didn't do anything special—just play video games, watch movies, or kick around the soccer ball or shoot hoops. Justin often explained that it was important to have his very close friends around him and that he needed to do normal teenage boy stuff.

Having those days off inevitably perked Justin up and refreshed him for the next round of music business.

Justin experienced a bit of nostalgia late in September when he returned to Canada to make an appearance on the season finale of the television series *The Next Star.* Returning to his roots, he thrilled the audience when he walked onstage, grinning from ear to ear, and performed acoustic versions of "One Less Lonely Girl" and "One Time." The Canadian press went wild over this brief return, but Justin downplayed the appearance, saying that it was something he wanted to do to give back to the fans in his home country.

Later in September, Justin returned to the big stage and belted out "One Time" for the umpteenth time on the MTV Video Music Awards Show concert. However, while his fairly short list of must-sing hits had resulted in him doing certain songs literally a hundred times, there was never a sign that he was not giving it his all. It was hard to get tired of doing something that brought him such joy and gave every new audience that first-time thrill. Justin had reasoned that being a pop star was glamorous work, but it was still work. And he also felt that it was a job that would never get old.

A big part of Justin's 2009 odyssey was centered around promoting the November 17 release of his first album, *My World*. The fact that half of the album's eight songs had already been released and were sizable commercial hits did not diminish the importance of *My World* being a smash. While he tended to leave the business side of the album's release to the adults, Justin was already savvy enough in the promotion game to talk about the esthetic side of the upcoming release.

"There's a lot of stuff that's not just about love," he told an MTV reporter. "There's songs that teens can relate to. Real life isn't perfect and my album kind of portrays that."

However, real life also meant maximum exposure in the now critical run-up to the album's release, which meant an October 12 appearance on *The Today Show*. The very adult-oriented daily morning news and interview program had also managed to attract a younger audience with regular live performances by up-and-coming musical stars, performed on the plaza outside the show's studios in Rockefeller Plaza. *Today Show* performances regularly drew audiences in the thousands.

But when it was announced, that Justin would be performing on the show it immediately became evident that this would not be a typical *Today Show* performance.

Young girls from all over the country began descending on New York City. By Saturday night, more than 32 hours before the Monday-morning performance, groups of girls were seen camping out on the sidewalk in front of the *Today Show* studios, in an attempt to be as close as possible when Justin hit the stage.

When Justin heard the news, he was amazed, and appreciative of the support and loyalty his fans had for him—so much so that on the night before the show, he put on a pair of dark glasses and a sweatshirt and went down to the site to mingle with his fans. Girls were shocked and surprised when Justin rounded a streetcorner. He willingly posed for cell phone pictures, signed autographs, and thanked his fans for showing up. The adults who monitored Justin's life had been a bit uneasy about Justin venturing out in the open. They knew how excited his fans could get and their worst fears were that he might be overpowered or injured. Happily, their fears were unfounded and the girls who had that unexpected, special meeting with their idol came away with memories that would last a lifetime.

For Justin, meeting with crowds of adoring and occasionally aggressive fans had been a learning curve. Always fan-friendly and willing to go the extra mile for them, he would occasionally balk when his security team would get between him and his admirers. Slowly but surely, however, he was coming to realize that security was there for his protection and that, even though he didn't always like it, he would have to trust their instincts because they knew more about such matters than he did.

Security for *Today* had been increased with the expectation of larger than normal crowds, and it turned out to be a good idea. The crowd had grown to several thousand by the time Justin took the stage. The expected pandemonium followed. There was some pushing and shoving and, at certain points, it looked like the wooden barricades would not be strong enough to hold the crowd back.

Justin rolled out the hits that cold but sunny morning, doing acoustic versions of "One Time," "One Less Lonely Girl," and "Favorite Girl," before waving to the crowd and walking off to thunderous applause.

By October 2009, Justin had logged thousands of miles on the road to stardom. As he climbed into the van that would wisk him off to the next show and the next appearance, he knew there was a lot more that had to be done. But if anyone was looking for one moment that defined how far and how fast Justin's life and career had come, one need look no farther than the *Today Show* performance.

It was indeed a moment captured in time.

8. AND OH...
BY THE WAY

When Justin was not running around the world, promoting himself and his music, there was the little matter of a follow-up album to deal with.

It was always a given that Def Jam wanted to strike while the iron was hot, and as soon as the last track on *My World* had been mastered, they started putting together the creative pieces for its successor, *My World 2.0,* which the record company had already scheduled to come out early in 2010, five months to the day after the release of the first album.

Among those invited back to collaborate on the second CD were producers/songwriters "Tricky" Stewart, The-Dream, and Midi Mafia. Welcomed aboard for the first time were Bryan-Michael Cox, the Stereotypes, the

Messengers, Melvin Hough II, Arden Altimo, and Dapo Torimiro.

But rather than more of the same, *My World 2.0* was already being conceived as a musical step forward for Justin. Something a bit more edgy. A bit more street. And nobody was more excited about that than Justin. He remarked that a quick second album was a good idea from a fan point of view because his fans did not want to wait a year or more for new music. As to the change in sound, he told the *Houston Chronicle*, "I wanted to do something that was a little more rhythm-and-blues, something that could reach out to everyone."

What was not said was that Justin, because he was a Def Jam artist, had become very immersed in the hip-hop genre and was friendly with many of its performers. What Justin and those around him were looking for was a little street cred.

Despite the nearly nonstop schedule of promotion and performing, Justin was always able to break away for some studio time. And when he was in the studio, he was all business. Tracks were locked down quickly. Justin was a fountain of ideas when it came to the songwriting process and was given due credit on all ten of the *My World 2.0* songs.

"Baby" was the song that everybody hoped would break Justin out of the teen heartthrob mold. For starters, the song was not the expected ballad; it was an upbeat, dance groove with Justin singing above it, with convincing rhythm-and-blues vocals. But the key for the producers was a guest rap at midpoint in the song by rap superstar Ludacris. There were those in the industry who worried that Ludacris might hurt his own street cred by appearing on a Justin Bieber song. But Ludacris had gotten to know Justin in the last year (both live in Atlanta) and did not think twice when Justin and Def Jam came up with the idea of his collaborating on "Baby," and he stepped on in.

However, Ludacris knew going in that working on a Justin Bieber song would present its own set of challenges. "I had to dig deep for the lyrics," he told MTV. "I just had to figure out how to be on a record with a fifteen-year-old. That's when I figured, 'Let me reminisce about the past.' As soon as I heard it, I knew it was going to be a hit."

Justin would go old-school on the song "U Smile," a very sweet, retro, Motown-style ballad. In an interview with MTV, Justin likened the song to payback. "I wrote it for all my fans who got me here."

Those in the studio were happily surprised that Justin had adjusted quickly to the requirements of much edgier songs. Yes, he was still a teenager. But he was also a quick study and, given the fact that he had grown up on a fairly steady diet of Stevie Wonder, Boyz II Men, and other soul standards, he was spot-on and was giving evidence that he had soul in his heart.

Nevertheless, the sessions did not entirely leave pure pop behind. The song "Somebody to Love," influenced

by Chris Brown's singing style, was very much in the tradition of the romantic pop ballads of the previous album.

Once again flexing his talents as a roots-oriented singer,
Justin in tandem with singer Sean Kingston, took to the
streets with "Eenie Meenie." The song quite literally had
everything—reggae, rhythm-and-blues, pop, and rap—
and perhaps more than just about any other song on the
album, gave evidence of how far and in what directions
Justin's music might travel. But while Justin would sometimes contemplate where he could go creatively, when he
wasn't in the studio recording *My World 2.0,* he had only
one thing on his mind . . .

The next city. The next show. The next place where
his fans would be waiting.

9. MORE VIDEOS, PLEASE

A lot of people who heard the songs on *My World 2.0* well in advance of the album's release had widely differing opinions. Some thought it was in keeping with the formula established with *My World*. Others speculated that it was a leap into slightly tougher musical territory, and one or two said the new music was downright dark.

Def Jam wasn't sure about how "Baby" would be greeted by radio stations. The song, which features the much-talked-about and slightly controversial contribution of Ludacris, would be the first single. A music video was certainly in order. The big question was how to create something that did not cast Justin in a harsh light and, at the same time, showcase Justin's new musical direction.

One thing was certain: "Baby" was going to be a spare-no-expense video. For openers, Ray Kay was brought in to direct. Kay had become the go-to guy in recent years, after a long string of video credits that included Beyoncé and Lady Gaga. Casting also took a high profile. It was a given that Ludacris would be on board to do his rap. Singer/actress Jasmine Villegas was cast as Justin's love interest. Also making appearances would be Young Money, Drake, and Lil Twist.

On the surface, the story seemed tried-and-true Justin. Justin and his girl break up, he decides he wants her back, she's not interested, and he spends the rest of video trying to convince her to make up. In the end he succeeds and they walk off hand in hand at the fade. However, Kay had some ideas to spice things up.

"Baby" was being compared by many to Michael Jackson's classic track "The Way You Make Me Feel," and it was decided that the video—played out in a bowling alley and other mall-like locations and filmed in late January 2010 at Universal City Walk—should have that similar feel. Choreography would be a major element, with Justin executing moves that were in keeping with Jackson's classic clip. Of course the ever playful Justin could not resist throwing in his own homage to the original and, at one point in the filming, executed a near perfect bit of Moonwalk for the occasion.

Ludacris was shedding his tough street cred with this song and, in the video, played the perfect rapping counterpoint to the piece. Justin seemed at his most comfortable during the filming, mugging and laughing off-camera and, sometimes, on.

The "Baby" video would ultimately prove retro in the best possible way; a very eighties vibe set in 2010. When it premiered on February 19, most people made the Michael Jackson connection and liked what they saw. In record time it would rise to the fifteenth most-viewed video in the history of YouTube and prove that bigger was most certainly better.

And then there was the very romantic kiss that was filmed during the making of "Baby," but which you never saw. At one point in the story line, the director felt it would be a nice touch if Justin and Jasmine kissed. What seemed like a good idea at the time was ultimately cut. But in an article that appeared on the Disney Dreaming Web site, Jasmine recalled, "The kiss was awesome. It was sweet. There was nothing awkward about it. We both knew that it was for the work."

So much had already been made of Justin's personal and romantic life that it seemed like a good opportunity to tease the fans a little bit. The proposed second single from *My World 2.0,* "Never Let You Go," proved to be the perfect way to do that. Filmed on location in the Bahamas, under the hand of first-time director Colin Tilley, the video showed Justin at his most mature romantically while keeping that pure, puppy-love vibe.

The concept of two teens falling in love in an exotic locale seemed the right way to go, and actress Paige Hurd (from the *Everybody Hates Chris* TV series) was ideal as Justin's love interest. The concept worked, and was enhanced by a series of scenes in which Justin and his girlfriend nearly kiss, and touch and nuzzle each other as they play on the beach and in other Bahamas locales. For the fans it was a deeper glimpse into the romantic ideal that Justin had been presenting.

The video treatment for "Eenie Meenie" presented some challenges. It was the first duet for Justin, with Sean Kingston, and while the chemistry between the pair had been perfect, creating a story line that gave both stars equal face time could be difficult. As difficult as it appeared at first, the narrative turned out to be quite simple.

Taking off on the nursery rhyme "eenie, meenie, miny, moe," the video presents a modern-day story of flirtation. Justin and Sean are hanging out at a Hollywood pool party. One moment a beautiful girl is flirting with Sean while Justin is off by himself. The next moment the same girl is flirting with Justin while Sean is now alone. As the pop-style song plays out, the girl goes back and forth between the two guys without either of them knowing what's going on. Near the conclusion of the video, the girl is with Sean when Justin walks in and catches them. In the end, the guys remain friends and each ends up with another girl.

Ray Kay was once again at the helm and produced a crisp, glitzy visual effect. The supporting cast includes Christian Beadles (Justin's long-rumored real-life ex), a return appearance by Jasmine Villegas, and the rapper Lil Romeo.

Obviously these are not the only videos of Justin on the Internet. Hundreds of performance and interview clips are available. They remain fun to watch and give viewers a comprehensive idea of what Justin is about.

But what the professional videos of Justin's singles have proven is that Justin is more than ready to play in the big leagues.

10. NO REST FOR THE TALENTED

November 1 is usually the time of year when most people are preparing for the holidays. Thanksgiving looms up ahead. Christmas is not far behind. But for Justin, the last thing on his mind was the holidays. *My World*, his first album, was set to be released in a few weeks and the only things on his plate were appearances and performances.

And sickness.

The constant traveling, long hours, and lack of good sleep had begun to wear on Justin. His skin appeared pale. More often than not, he was looking tired and worn. It was inevitable that occasionally he would get sick.

The first time Justin went public with an illness was on October 26 when Justin went Twitter happy in describing to his millions of fans that he was not feeling too well and was looking forward to his grandparents coming over with some chicken soup. A week later, another Justin tweet indicated that he was once again sick and that a scheduled November 1 show in Vancouver would have to be canceled.

Not surprisingly, fans took these reports very seriously. But while he usually bounced back from minor colds and the flu, it was a sign to those in his entourage that they would have to monitor Justin's health closely.

An interesting cross promotion between Justin and the clothing store Urban Behavior brought Justin back to Canada for the week of November 3–6. Those were essentially a meet-and-greet in Urban Behavior stores in Edmonton, Montreal, and London, followed by a show in Toronto, the November 3 appearance turned into an endurance test in which Justin started out the day in Los Angeles with an appearance on the popular daytime talk show *The Ellen DeGeneres Show* before flying up to Canada for the first of the in-store appearances.

Just when it reached a point where there were not enough hours in the day, and his mother was legitimately concerned that Justin badly needed a few days off, an offer too good to refuse was dropped in Justin's lap. Taylor Swift wanted to know if Justin was interested in opening for her at a couple of UK shows at the end of the month.

Justin and Taylor had become fast friends following their meeting at the VMAs. They tweeted and texted each

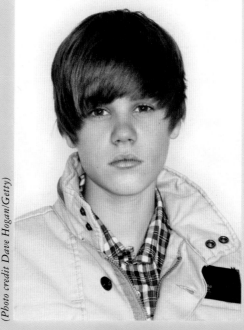

(Photo credit Dave Hogan/Getty)

(Photo credit Bryan Bedder/Getty)

VISITING THE NINTENDO WORLD STORE.

JUSTIN WITH
SELENA GOMEZ
AT DICK CLARK'S
NEW YEAR'S
ROCKIN' EVE WITH
RYAN SEACREST
2010.

(Photo credit Kevin Winter/DCNYRE2010/Getty)

PERFORMING ON
NBC'S "TODAY"
NEW YORK,
OCTOBER 12, 2009.

(Photo credit Andrew H. Walker/Getty)

SPEAKING WITH WHOOPI GOLDBERG AND BARBARA WALTERS **ON ABC'S "THE VIEW."**

WITH ACTRESS VICTORIA JUSTICE at THE NICKELODEON 2010 UPFRONT PRESENTATION.

PERFORMING ON NBC'S "TODAY" ON OCTOBER 12, 2009.

(Photo credit Bryan Bedder/Getty)

(Photo credit Theo Wargo/Getty)

JUSTIN LIGHTS THE
EMPIRE STATE
BUILDING
FOR READ FOR THE
RECORD DAY.

(Photo credit Mike Coppola/Getty)

BACKSTAGE WITH
RIHANNA
AT THE 52ND
ANNUAL GRAMMY
AWARDS.

(Photo credit Michael Buckner/Getty)

WITH ACTRESS MIRANDA COSGROVE AT THE NICKELODEON 2010 UPFRONT PRESENTATION.

AT THE LAUNCH OF VEVO, A MUSIC-VIDEO WEBSITE, ON DECEMBER 8, 2009 IN NEW YORK CITY.

(Photo credit Bryan Bedder/Getty)

WITH USHER
AT Z100'S JINGLE BALL
2009 SHOW.

PERFORMING
ON ABC'S "THE VIEW."

(Photo credit Jason LaVeris/Getty)

(Photo credit Steve Fenn/Getty)

PEREZ HILTON POSES WITH JUSTIN
AT PEREZ HILTON'S "CARN-EVIL" THEATRICAL
FREAK AND FUNK 32ND BIRTHDAY PARTY.

VISITING LIVE AT MUCHMUSIC, TORONTO, ONTARIO.

(Photo credit George Pimentel/Getty)

other on a regular basis. And they had long since become fans of each other's music. In fact, Taylor regularly listened to Justin's music when she had a rare quiet moment. When it appeared that neither of her current opening acts, Kellie Pickler and Gloriana, would be available for the two UK shows, she immediately thought of Justin.

Justin wouldn't need a lot of rehearsal time to get a full set up to speed for those shows. He was already doing his show, or at least a big part of it, at just about every appearance.

The personal appearances continued. He did the TV show *Good Morning America* and countless press interviews in the space of three days. It is safe to say that Justin was more bored than tired at this point. The show formats were identical. In fact, change the faces of the hosts and they all could have been the exact same show. But Justin good-naturedly jumped through the hoops.

He did the bit of chitchat with adult hosts who were so unhip that, even at this point, the best they could do was offer up the same questions he had heard a thousand times before. Consequently, Justin was more mechanical in his responses than he had been months earlier. Then it was time to sing a song. Afterward, it was out the door and into the waiting crowds of hysterical fans. And one thing Justin was discovering, possibly as a result of his doing the day-time talk-show rounds, was that there were a lot of mothers who had come along to experience Bieber Fever with their daughters and sometimes it got downright embarrassing.

.They would often scream longer and louder than their daughters. Outrageous comments from the parents were not uncommon. Like the one mother who screamed out that her daughter was available for a playdate if Justin was interested, while her mortified daughter cringed a few steps away. Outbursts like that led Pattie to remark in a *New York Times* interview, "The parents were the worst."

November 2009 would also be notable for the first time Justin stepped in front of a camera and took a shot at acting. Because he proved to be a natural on the talk-show circuit, the possibility of his appearing in movies and television was being discussed. A very serious rumor was afoot that a script was being written that could mark Justin's first film role.

Justin was more than willing to play along with the rumor and, on more than one occasion, had indicated he would like to give acting a try at some point. The rumor became a reality in early November, when Justin agreed to do a guest-starring role on the season premiere episode of the Nickelodeon comedy series *True Jackson*. The episode, entitled "True Concert," had a simple premise: Justin would play himself.

As the episode unfolds, True and her friends sneak into a recording studio and watch as Justin records the song "One Time." They attempt to get close to their idol by walking into the studio and pretending to deliver a pizza. When Justin opens the box and finds it's empty, he summons his security team and has True and her friends tossed out. That the episode was set to air November 17, the day of the release of *My World,* was pure icing on the cake.

The guest spot was more of a lark for Justin than anything else, but those who saw the scenes being shot had to admit that he was comfortable in front of the camera and had the potential to go far as an actor. Justin admitted it was a possibility during a *Teen Vogue* interview. "We're trying to set up a movie for me in the near future," he said. "It's going to be similar to the story of how I got discovered."

November 17 was Bieber Day nationally and internationally for the release of Justin's debut album. Lines were forming outside stores hours in advance, in anticipation of the official release. But for Justin in Los Angeles, it was just another day at the office.

After an early rise and his usual three hours of schooling, Justin was off for a final round of talk-show appearances. First it was *Lopez Tonight* with comedian George Lopez, whose hipness to pop culture made it one of Justin's more enjoyable appearances.

Later in the day it was an unprecedented second visit in two weeks to *The Ellen DeGeneres Show,* where, in a good-natured moment, he showed he could dance as well as sing. He was barely finished with Ellen when he was whisked off to nearby Universal Studios to attend a spe-

cial album release and performance party for a select audience who had been lucky enough to purchase specially
marked copies of *My World*.

Justin was euphoric as he hopped a plane and headed
east for another round of press interviews. He was in such
a good mood that when it was suggested that he do a short
notice store signing in a Long Island, New York, mall, he
readily agreed to it. Everybody around Justin figured it
was another way to give back to the fans. It would create
publicity. And it would be easy.

What, they reasoned, could possibly go wrong?

11. Break A Leg

Justin was shook up after the riot at the Roosevelt Field Mall. Dumbfounded at the idea that the police would threaten to take him to jail if he showed up at the mall. Amazed that Braun had been arrested and charged with contributing to the riot by failing to send out a tweet telling the crowd to disperse. Justin had gotten used to the hysterical fans who would scream and holler and run after him. Things had been close to getting out of hand before, but this was the first time they actually had.

However, Justin's spirits were lifted by the instant, overwhelming success of *My World*. The album debuted at 6 on the *Billboard* charts, selling a phenomenal 127,000 copies in its first week. It also immediately charted in Canada and a number of countries in Europe and Asia.

My World went gold within the first month and platinum two months later.

Despite his worldwide popularity, it was expected that critical opinion, which in the past has often been unkind to teen artists, would be mixed at best in reviews of *My World*. However, reviewers, even when their comments were tepid, tended to find something they liked about Justin's debut.

The Toronto Star described the album as "a young Chris Brown with overdubbed New Edition–style harmonies." *Entertainment Weekly*, despite weighing in with only a B– rating, did acknowledge that "the song 'Love Me' [had] killer electro glam groove." And *Billboard* raved, "The vocals are as boyish as they are disarmingly mature."

Shortly after the release of *My World*, Justin hopped a flight to London and began making preparations for the Taylor Swift shows. It was an exciting time, hanging out with Taylor, doing a little bit of press, seeing some of the sights of London, and having all the excitement of being a young kid in a foreign land.

Justin went to Wembley Stadium in London on the day of the show for a sound check. Looking out on the empty stadium that would soon house 12,000 delirious fans only added to the emotion of the moment. As the opening act, Justin had come up with a compact song list for his set: six originals and a cover of Chris Brown's "With You." There had been talks about Taylor joining Justin on stage for an encore and Justin returning the favor at the conclusion of Taylor's set. But nobody was saying for sure.

Backstage that night, it was all high energy, with musicians and crew excitedly milling around while respective entourages flitted about, making sure their stars were relaxed and happy. Amid the controlled chaos, Justin and Taylor were finding time to make small talk and joke. In the rapidly filling stadium, the excitement level of the crowd was rising.

Finally, the house lights dimmed and Justin's band and backup dancers got ready to go on stage. Justin and Taylor shared a hug. And she laughingly offered the traditional theatrical slogan . . .

Break a leg.

Screams greeted Justin as he walked on stage. The band hit the first musical notes and Justin's UK set was off and running.

Justin was on top of his game, strutting the stage like a pro and giving the screaming audience an electrifying mixture of pure pop music mixed with oh-so-much soul. Everything was going along pretty much as expected as Justin reached the next to last song in his set, when he made a false step during an intricate dance move, tripped, and fell.

Justin immediately picked himself up and, with a sheepish grin on his face, continued the song as if nothing had happened. But the reality was that, at that moment, he was in a lot of pain. Justin went right into the final song,

"One Time." He was giving it his best shot to finish on a high note but it was obvious to concerned onlookers backstage that something was wrong. Justin finished the song and limped gingerly offstage. There was an encore song built into his set but, as he hobbled over to the near- est chair and collapsed into it, it was clear there would be no encore tonight.

Medics were summoned and did a preliminary exami- nation of Justin's foot. It was painful to the touch and discolored. An ambulance was called and, as those back- stage watched with concern, Justin was loaded into it and driven to the nearest hospital.

It was an uncomfortable night. X-rays revealed that the fall had fractured his foot. It was put in a cast. The next day, he was able to hobble around his hotel room on a lighter air-cast. Given the circumstances, nobody would have blamed Justin if he decided it was impossible to per- form the following night in Manchester. But Justin in- sisted that he could do it and so, when the time came, he carefully walked out to the center of the stage and sat down on a stool. From that position, he performed his entire set and then walked off to a standing ovation.

After a short press jaunt through Europe, Justin re- turned to the States. The talk-show appearances and press interviews had now become a blur. But occasionally one would pique his interest, in this instance, the December 13 taping of the annual *Christmas in Washington* television spe- cial that would air on December 20. Justin was excited about this show for several reasons. First, it was a charity event that would benefit the National Children's Medical Center. Also he would have the opportunity to meet President Barack Obama and his wife, Michelle. Finally, he would be part of a group of superstar performers that included Mary J. Blige, Neil Diamond, Sugarland, Rob Thomas, and, of particular interest, his mentor, Usher.

For the occasion, Justin sang a heartfelt rendition of Stevie Wonder's "Someday at Christmas." He reported that the President and First Lady "were cool."

"It was amazing," elaborated Justin on the Web site 4 Music. "It was incredible and the President was really nice. And I guess I was a bit nervous."

However, Justin laughingly recalled in *People* that a minor misstep occurred when the President mispronounced his name. "Yeah, he messed up my name but I give it to him. He's not the age category I sing to."

Justin flew back to Los Angeles for a free concert that brought out thousands. Fans noticed that, despite stories that he had performed without the leg cast the previous day for the President, the cast was now back on. Justin would later tweet that the cast was supposed to come off the previous week but that he kept it on for the Obama concert. He also assured fans that while the foot did not hurt anymore, his mother was still upset.

Christmas in Washington was the unofficial kickoff of the holiday season. It was a time when many big concerts and holiday specials with superstar acts were regularly held.

Justin was about the hottest star in the celebrity sky at the time and was actively pursued by those looking for his kind of celebrity power to end the year.

Easily the biggest show of the lot was the annual Z100 Jingle Ball at New York City's Madison Square Garden. The lineup consisted of some real heavy hitters, including Taylor Swift, John Mayer, *American Idol* favorites Jordin Sparks and Kris Allen, Pitbull, and a host of others. Justin had not completely recovered from his accident in London and was still hobbling around in a walking cast. But this was an opportunity he was not about to pass up.

Screams for Justin began reverberating through the massive hall even before the first act went on. Despite an all-star lineup, it was obvious who the fans were most excited about. As the show progressed, false alarms were shouted out with just about every announcement. During Jordin Sparks's set, Justin finally made an appearance, limping out to do a duet with the singer on "No Air."

Justin came out for his own set at 10:20 PM to a deafening roar from the crowd. His injured foot limited his stage presence somewhat but the charisma he radiated with each song more than made up for it. He did three songs before Usher sauntered onto the stage, and mentor and student performed a duet on Usher's "U Got It Bad." Justin finished his set with a rendition of "One Time" before moving off-stage to thunderous applause. The Jingle Ball was the best kind of Christmas present. In a star-studded lineup, Justin shone the brightest of all in a truly magical moment.

As the biggest year any fifteen-year-old could possibly experience began to wind down, Justin was finding himself in a contemplative mood. He would regularly tell interviewers that being around adults all the time had given him a new kind of maturity but that, in many ways, he was still immature. He constantly felt thankful for his success but was quick to point out that there was still a lot of work to be done.

His final event for 2009 would be a prime spot on what had become an annual television event, *Dick Clark's New Year's Rockin' Eve* extravaganza, held in Las Vegas. Presented by Ryan Seacrest and Dick Clark and hosted by Fergie, this years' star-studded lineup would also include the Black Eyed Peas, fellow teen star Selena Gomez, and Robin Thicke. Justin already had it in mind that he would do "One Time" at this performance. But during rehearsals for the show, he and Selena Gomez came up with an idea for something special for his follow-up number, "One Less Lonely Girl."

On the night of the show, Justin appeared on the huge, amazingly lit outdoor Vegas stage and was greeted by thousands of young girls screaming his name. He had already witnessed this response countless times but this night, set against the Vegas glitz and glamour, it all seemed a bit surreal. Justin immediately took command of the stage. With his foot now completely healed, his dance steps and showstopping choreography were electric. His voice was by now a trademark mixture of pop and R&B

stylings. He had sung "One Time" too often to count over the past year, but one could sense, amid the New Year's Eve excitement, a polish and charisma that made the now-familiar tune something special.

Justin launched into his second number, "One Less Lonely Girl." The rehearsals with Selena paid off, as halfway through the song she came onstage and Justin addressed the poignant lyrics to her, with an added dramatic flair. She then joined Justin's backup dancers for a moving finale to the song.

Justin could not be happier. The show marked a satisfying climax to a truly unbelievable year. However, he was anxious to see what would come next. His feeling was: Bring on 2010. Because he was ready for it.

12. IN DEMAND

Justin eased into 2010 on the wings of change.

On the surface things may have appeared the same. He was the center of a screaming teen girl universe. The poster boy for *Tiger Beat, Bop,* and countless other teen idol publications. Yet slowly but surely, the world outside was starting to get hip.

Perhaps taking a cue from *Billboard*'s early, deeper coverage of Justin's rise to stardom and all that it entailed, *Rolling Stone,* which regularly turns a blind eye to what they consider unimportant music, wrote about Justin in a January issue. Not that they were able to do much more then reiterate the narrative that everybody already seemed to know. But to those on the inside, just being featured in *Rolling Stone* was a giant step toward legitimacy. Likewise, traditional daily newspapers such as the *Los Angeles Times* and *The New York Times* also ventured into Justin's universe and covered it from every possible angle.

And one of those angles centered on the speculation that Justin was mostly a product of public relations and hype, and that once the hysteria died down he, like teen idols of the past, would ultimately sink or swim on the strength of his talent.

Justin had been hearing those kinds of remarks almost from the beginning, but in an interview with CTV-W5, he remained confident that he was in it for the long haul. "Five years down the road, I see myself furthering my career and winning a Grammy."

While Justin may have been a bit self-indulgent in predicting Grammy glory, those in charge of garnering the widest possible audience for the yearly Grammy telecast already knew about Justin's popularity and his ability to draw viewers. On January 14, it was announced that Justin had agreed to join the impressive list of presenters for the January 31 awards show. Justin greeted the news with typical youthful enthusiasm. But for those around him, it was definitely a sign that the young singer was on the music industry's radar.

After a couple of days off following his New Year's Eve appearance, Justin was once again on the promotion trail. With *My World* barely out of the box, Justin was also faced with having to get the good word out on *My World 2.0,* which was scheduled for a March release.

Much like the release pattern of the first CD, Def Jam had decided to prime the pump with a January release of the first single from *My World 2.0*. On January 18, "Baby" made its debut as a digital download on iTunes before its national radio release on January 26. The result was predictably amazing. "Baby" debuted at 5 on the *Billboard* charts, and to unanimously positive reviews.

About.com's critics said, "Bieber sings as well as Michael Jackson at that age. The lyrics are pitched perfectly in reference to young love." *Billboard* opined, "The midtempo number's contagious chorus should keep Bieber's fans satisfied." *Rap-Up* magazine stated, "The sweet pop fare gets a little street cred courtesy of Ludacris."

After a quick, one-day jaunt to the UK for a round of promotion, where he found himself constantly surrounded by teenage girls, Justin returned to the States for another stab at acting. The School Gyrls were a pop-music trio who, unlike Justin, had found a home with Nickelodeon and managed to turn it into a recording contract, a comic book, and a series of young adult novels. It seemed only natural that they should do a movie and even more natural that Justin should be in it. Make no mistake, Justin's appearance in the film was nothing more than a cameo. But even in this small moment, it reinforced his ease in front of a camera.

Justin ended an already busy January with his appearance at the Grammys. Despite being used to the idea of awards shows and being around top-of-the-line stars, Justin, who presented the award for Best New Artist with another rising star, Ke$ha, found himself in awe of being included among pop music's elite on this night. However, being a normal teenager, Justin let anyone who would listen know that he was particularly on the lookout for Beyoncé.

Following the Grammys, Justin turned his attention to doing some charity work. The recent earthquake in Haiti had resonated deeply in the pop-music community. On the eve of the twenty-fifth anniversary of the recording of the song "We Are the World," some of the biggest names in the music business had decided to record an updated version, with all the proceeds going to Haiti relief. Justin was honored to be asked to join in and, in particular, to sing the introductory lines to the song, which had originally been done by Lionel Richie.

Justin was anxious as he walked through the door of Henson Studios in Los Angeles, and with good reason. He had been told that a total of eighty-one superstars had agreed to participate. A few names had been bandied about, and what he heard had excited him. But nothing could have prepared him for the scene inside the sprawling soundstage.

Off in one corner was the legendary songstress Barbra Streisand. In another was Kanye West and Lil Wayne. Jostling for position in the recording area and fiddling with microphones were Nick Jonas, LL Cool J, and

Celine Dion. Carlos Santana, Rob Thomas, Toni Braxton. Just about everywhere Justin looked he saw one of his idols.

Justin huddled with the session producer, Lionel Richie. Having drawn a plumb assignment for the session, singing the opening stanzas, there were nerves. But as the session unfolded, Justin instantly felt at ease taking the solo spotlight before sliding back into the overall group sound. Hours later, the session was completed. Justin was speechless, overwhelmed by the experience and very much a little kid as he would attempt to explain his feelings to journalists at the conclusion of this landmark recording.

"The experience was out of this world," he offered to MTV and others. "It was amazing. It was incredible!"

And the consensus from those who worked with him on "We Are the World" was that he definitely had his act together. The song's video director, veteran filmmaker Paul Haggis, reitereated what others had said, that Justin was a natural in front of the camera. Nick Jonas was equally complimentary in a *Calgary Sun* interview. "I think he's doing a good job so far. It's interesting to see the path that he's on."

On February 4, immediately after the "We Are the World" sessions, Justin and his entourage flew to Miami where, in another sign of his growing popularity, he had been asked to perform as part of the Super Bowl pregame show. Being very athletic and sports-oriented, Justin got a kick out of singing outside in the sunshine at the biggest sports event of the year, and he responded with an enthusiastic performance.

Justin continued his good works on the Haiti front the next day, when he joined another stellar lineup to both perform and work the phones for the BET: Saving Ourselves—Help for Haiti benefit concert. The event, which also featured the likes of Wyclef Jean, Ludacris, Chris Brown, and Mary J. Blige, featured Justin doing a set of his hits which included "Baby" and "I'll Never Let You Go" from the upcoming *My World 2.0*. Justin proved equally adept at working the phones and he had to admit it was kind of funny. People calling in to make donations would recognize Justin on the other end of the line and instantly burst into hysterical screams.

The smile never left Justin's face. Part of it was the experience and part of it was just being able to help.

13. THERE'S A RIOT GOING ON

Justin was now officially a worldwide sensation. Music journalists indicated that his popularity in the United States and Canada had, in many cases, been surpassed by that of London, Paris, Japan, and South America. When it came time to crank up the promotion wagon for yet another round of appearances to publicize the upcoming release of *My World 2.0,* international stops figured heavily into the schedule.

One of the first would be Paris. Justin was excited at the prospect. It would be the first time that he would appear in a country where language was an issue and he was curious to see how his appeal differed in a non–English speaking country. He was also looking forward to picking up a few French words along the way.

Justin and his entourage landed in Paris on February 21. Judging from the enthusiastic reception he received at the airport by fans and paparazzi alike, the French could not wait to meet their idol. Almost immediately, Justin was thrust into a whirlwind of press interviews and radio-station appearances. The questions were still familiar, but coming as they were from a French perspective, Justin was far from bored and totally upbeat. Part of the reason for his good nature was the fact that later in the day he would be doing a meet-and-greet at the famed Citadium store for what was predicted to be a couple thousand fans.

But what Justin's people and the local authorities failed to realize was that Justin Bieber fans were not to be trifled with.

Long before his scheduled appearance, thousands of fans had already crammed into the store, filling it to over-flowing. But that did not stop an ever increasing stream of fans from continuing to push and shove their way in, packing the store like sardines. Not surprisingly, the French police had underestimated the size of the crowd and were beginning to panic. The situation was made more precarious when the van carrying Justin pulled up in front of the store. Flimsy barricades were pushed forward as fans attempted to get at their hero, who could barely be seen behind a wall of large security guards. It was a claustrophobic situation, to say the least, which could not have sat very well with Justin's known fear of tight places.

In a tweet to his fans, reported in countless outlets including Aceshowbiz, Justin would explain what happened next.

"There were thousands of kids in the store and the police were not expecting it. Finally, they reorganized it and we got it going. But after a while, the police came in, said it was over, and that I had to leave."

The store was quickly emptied out. Many of the fans who had not been able to meet Justin were mingling around outside the store and they were not happy. Some were making negative comments about Justin. Justin was not surprised. He had long ago been taught that when fans are disappointed, they will often lash out at their idol, believing that he was the one responsible for their disappointment. But as always, Justin attempted to soothe their hurt feelings with a tweet.

"Paris is crazy," said the tweet, as reported by Aceshowbiz and others. "Sorry to any of the kids I did not get to meet. I love all of you for your support."

Justin would attempt to make it up to the fans the next day when he did a free concert from the first-floor window of the Universal Music building in Paris. The crowd, as expected, was massive but, in comparison to the previous day, at least a bit more under control.

There were a lot of cameras following Justin around Paris. But it was not only the usual paparazzi and their blinding flash guns. Prior to the trip to Paris, Justin and his management team had struck a deal with MTV, which had been an early and vigorous supporter of Justin from the beginning, to shoot a documentary of Justin's exploits in Paris and New York, to be called *Diary of Justin Bieber.*

The documentary followed Justin through a typical business day, rare down time, and the growing hysteria. However, the scope of the documentary went much farther than just another excuse to see Justin's smiling face in different locales and situations. According to producer Andrew Huang, the idea was to capture Justin in a moment in time that we would never see again. In Huang's eyes, Justin was already a big star but he could still walk down the street and act fairly normal in the face of stardom. But the consensus was that those days were about to end and that the coming superstardom would change his life forever.

Justin returned to the States apparently none the worse for the Paris experience. He was more than happy to swing by Philadelphia radio station Q102 on March 8 for an appearance at the longtime supportive station. The idea was to avoid publicizing the event and to visit and leave the station without hype or hysteria.

Unfortunately, Justin chose that moment to have a major lapse in judgment.

The always fan-friendly performer decided the appearance would be better with his fans around and so he tweeted exactly when and where he would be. News spread, and when Justin's van rounded the corner and stopped in front of the radio station, all hell broke loose.

A mob of young girls rushed the van, cell phones snapping away and fans pushing and shoving their way toward

Justin. None of this was unusual at a Justin appearance but there was a sense that this crowd was more out of control than usual. With a wall of security guards in front of him, Justin sidestepped the arms reaching for him and managed to make it to the studio's door and inside.

Justin did a short interview and, as the sound of screaming girls reached a fever pitch, stepped to the window of the radio station. The mere sight of Justin waving and smiling down on the crowd sent them into an uncontrollable frenzy. With the interview concluded, Justin's entourage was all set to sneak Justin out a side door and into the van for a quick getaway. But the ever-friendly Justin insisted on going out the way they came, into the teeth of the crowd, to meet his fans on an up-close-and-personal level.

This would prove to be a big mistake.

The moment the door opened, Justin and his security guards were faced with the fight of their lives. The crowd of young girls stormed the small boy, grabbing frantically at his hair and body, shoving people out of the way, and screaming at the top of their lungs. The look on Justin's face suddenly changed. It was not his perpetually smiling face.

Justin looked scared to death.

The crowd surged forward as Justin and his guards inched toward the van. At one point, Justin's mother, who had been screaming in the face of the mob, started crying. From somewhere in the madness, somebody in Justin's entourage yelled, "Are you all right, little buddy?" One look at Justin's face told the whole story.

No, he was not.

They finally made it to the van. Justin and his mother jumped in. The van instantly began to inch forward. The crowd was completely out of control. Girls were pounding on the van windows. The van was rocking back and forth. At one point a girl jumped on the hood of the van and had to be peeled off by security. Finally, security managed to part the crowd and the van slid through the opening and out into the street.

Justin was staring straight ahead. Silent.

Nevertheless, nobody was more *happy* about the craziness surrounding Justin than Usher. In an interview with the Canadian press, he said, "How many Beatles-type artists do you have? Where he shuts down malls? When he goes out in public, the streets shut down. That's the type of business I wanted to be in. When I saw him, I just felt like, 'You know, this could be the one.'"

Moments like the Q102 incident made Justin think about the price of fame. And he acknowledged in a *Splash News* item that, at this point, he really looked forward to those moments away from the spotlight and being around people who could care less that he's a star.

"I miss hanging out with my friends," he said of lifelong Stratford buddies Ryan and Chaz. "I keep up with them through e-mails and texts. Sometimes they'll come out on the road for a day or two and we can just hang out and do normal stuff. I also like it that my mom is always with me. I really appreciate that when I'm waking up in a different country every day."

Justin barely had time to get used to Eastern Standard Time when he was once again on a plane crossing the Atlantic in late March. More of a business and press trip than a fan-friendly meet and greet, Justin, nevertheless, was almost immediately targeted by his fans. Paparazzi on motorcycles dogged him from the moment he landed in the UK. Masses of screaming girls milled around outside the Camden offices of MTV UK where Justin was conducting an interview. As soon as he emerged from the building they stormed the hastily erected barricades.

The next day, after a meeting with some people at BBC Radio, Justin stepped outside to again find a mass of young girls screaming and approaching fast. Justin jumped into the van and, as it began to inch its way through the crowd, he tossed candy to the girls in an attempt to distract them away from the van. Some in the crowd grumbled that the act was rude and cursed him under their breath. But all was forgiven later in the day when Justin sent out a tweet, alerting his fans that he would be taking a meeting with some record company people at the Mayfair Hotel and that he would like to greet them afterward.

Not surprisingly, thousands of screaming fans turned up at the Mayfair at the appointed hour. But Justin's security, rightfully cautious after what had recently happened in Paris and Philadelphia, decided, at the last minute, to sneak him out the side entrance and away. And they weren't taking no for an answer.

When word leaked out that Justin had already left, the girls were again upset at their idol and the curses leveled at him were loud and clear. Justin tried to soothe their feelings with an apologetic tweet to explain what had happened.

That night, Justin hung out with some of the UK music people and bent over backwards to be extra nice to those fans who were somehow able to breach his security and approach him. On the flight back to the States, Justin thought about the craziness, the fan disappointment, and all the things that went with being the biggest star on the planet.

But he had just turned sixteen. He was confident he could handle it.

14. IT'S MY PARTY

Justin was looking forward to doing all the things a sixteen-year-old can do. First of all, he would be able to get his driver's license and, he hoped, a car. But easily more important to the teenager was that he would now be allowed to date.

"My mother told me I could not date until I was sixteen," he said in a *People* magazine interview. "She thought I wasn't ready yet because I was too immature. But she said I would have her permission when I turned sixteen."

Justin knew that after working really hard for nearly two years, he was ready to blow off steam and make his sixteenth birthday a memorable one. He talked to his mother about it first. Pattie had to admit that her son's ideas for his party were extreme. But she also had to admit that he was in a position to make all his dreams possible.

And who was she to deny him? Justin had come to recognize pop stardom as a privilege and was always appreciative of what fame had done for him. He also gradually realized that, as long as he was not being totally unreasonable in his demands, he could pretty much get whatever he wanted, whenever he wanted it, just by asking. His requests had never been what one would consider outrageous and so, with his birthday in sight, his big dreams suddenly took flight.

How big those dreams were became known on the Internet and other media outlets in mid-February, when the particulars of Justin's party invitations, sent out to old friends, new friends, and important people in the music industry, were made public. What was planned as a three-day party held at a private Malibu estate, would begin with the arrival of guests and a lavish birthday dinner on February 27. February 28 would feature a private movie screening of *The Book of Eli*. March 1 would be the actual birthday bash, which would include a backyard pool-side barbecue, karaoke, sumo wrestling, laser tag, basketball, and air hockey, among other activities. The event would also offer guests such luxuries as an on-call chef, a gym, the use of a tennis court, and any number of video games.

With tongue planted firmly in cheek, the invitation included a waiver and release for those under the age of eighteen, stating that participation in this party may involve serious injury or death. But the reality of Justin's party was that it was going to be kid-friendly: no alcohol, cigarettes, or drugs allowed. Needless to say, word of the party spread like wildfire with fans trying to crash it at any cost. However, security was tight and only those with an invitation and proper ID made it in.

Pictures from the party quickly leaked out and what they showed was a happy Justin turning sixteen and showing signs of shedding his preteen image. He was all smiles by the pool, often surrounded by young girls in sexy two-piece swimsuits. The shyness had dissolved and his smiling face was a sure sign that he was getting older and more worldly.

Easily one of the high points of Justin's three-day party was the arrival of Usher, who brought down the house with his birthday gift, a brand-new Range Rover. Justin was beside himself with excitement. He was now old enough to drive, and he was old enough to date. Now, if he only had the time to do any of that.

Following his Malibu party, Justin flew to Toronto for a more intimate birthday party with his family and longtime friends. It was a different kind of affair. Nearly everybody there had known him before he had become famous and so the attitude was more relaxed and laid-back. Despite his notoriety, nearly everyone had memories of what Justin had been like growing up, the things he liked to do, and where he hung out. Justin appreciated having this kind of grounding, a connection to the time before the whole world knew his name.

But just as quickly, it was back to the new world that had become his world.

In keeping with the way the *My World* songs were released, the first cut from *My World 2.0,* "Never Let You Go," was released to iTunes on March 2 to the expected positive reviews and a tidal wave of hits.

The *Boston Herald* said, "The promises of forever will undoubtedly delight the young girls who dream of spending eternity with pop's newest heartthrob." *Rolling Stone* reported, "The ballad is fully realized, mixing love struck lyrics with big, lovable choruses."

For Justin, it was then back on yet another red-eye flight for another promotional jaunt on the other side of the world.

The first stop was Berlin, for The Dome 53 radio program on March 5. Justin was more than a little jetlagged but his spirits were raised when he was informed that back home he had been nominated in three different categories in the annual Canadian equivalent of the Grammys, the Junos. He was in the running for Album of the Year, Pop Album of the Year, and New Artist of the Year.

Then it was over to London, where he appeared on the top-rated talk show *Alan Carr: Chatty Man.* And it was shortly after leaving that show that Justin, who as a pop star was already a hero, suddenly found himself a hero in a much more real sense.

When Justin left the studio, he was immediately confronted with a familiar sight—a wall of screaming girls pushing hard against a barricade and security attempting to protect him. He was fine with that until he happened to look down and spot a young child, perhaps no more than three, who had somehow managed to wriggle to the front of the crowd. The child looked confused and a bit frightened. Suddenly the crowd pushed particularly hard and the child fell down. The crowd was looming over the child and would most certainly trample it. Justin did not have to think about what he did next. He reached down and lifted the child up into his arms just as the crowd surged in, saving it from injury or much worse.

The next day he was off to the popular morning talk show *GMTV*. During the interview he was asked whether or not he would ever consider dating a fan. Until now, that question was irrelevant, since he was not allowed to date, period. But since he had turned sixteen and his mother had given her son the okay, it was now a question worth contemplating.

"I don't know," he said on the show. "I think that it just depends on what the situation is. I'm not going to limit myself."

Justin was again highly visible on the charity front early in March, when he returned to Canada to help out

Haiti. As Canadian singer-songwriter K'naan had already had a hit single with the song "Wavin' Flag," it was suggested that a cover, with the proceeds going to Haiti relief, would be a good idea. Canadian stars rallied around the concept. Under the banner Young Artists for Haiti, Justin, along with such celebrity stalwarts as Nelly Furtado, Drake, and Avril Lavigne, among others, recorded the song during a quick session and happily watched as the song raised an incredible amount of money for Haiti relief.

Justin returned to the States and then, apparently more as a lark than anything else, appeared on the QVC Shopping Channel show *Q Sessions* to sing a few songs and do an awkward interview in an attempt to drum up presale orders for *My World 2.0*. That it came across to many as a total embarrassment did not seem to bother Justin or his handlers.

The QVC appearance was just another way of getting the word out that the release of *My World 2.0* was a mere three days away. Not that any reminder seemed necessary at that point. The Internet had been abuzz for some weeks in anticipation of the album's release. Some Web sites were literally counting down the weeks, days, and hours.

The second iTunes release, "U Smile," was made available March 16, three days before the album's release. Most critics seemed to understand the song's old-school sentiments but *Entertainment Weekly* summed it up best when their critic called the song "a shimmery slice of blue-eyed soul."

ARRIVING AT THE 52ND ANNUAL GRAMMY AWARDS.

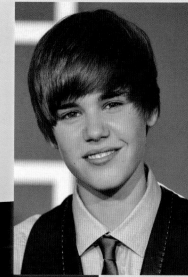

(Photo credit John Shearer/Getty)

(Photo credit Kevin Mazur/Getty)

BACKSTAGE WITH TAYLOR SWIFT AT Z100'S JINGLE BALL 2009.

PERFORMING WITH JORDIN SPARKS
AT Z100'S JINGLE BALL 2009.

◀ ⋯⋯⋯⋯⋯

POSING WITH THE JONAS BROTHERS AT THE 52ND ANNUAL GRAMMY AWARDS.

⋯⋯⋯⋯▶

PERFORMING AT THE PEPSI SUPER BOWL FAN JAM.

ARRIVING AT NICKELODEON'S 23RD ANNUAL KIDS' CHOICE AWARDS.

92.3 NOW'S
"BOWLING WITH BIEBER"
RECORD RELEASE PARTY.

A JUSTIN BIEBER
SIGHTING IN LONDON,
MARCH 18, 2010.

POSING WITH FERGIE BACKSTAGE AT THE GRAMMY AWARDS.

(Photo credit Lester Cohen/Getty)

PERFORMING AT THE NICKELODEON UPFRONTS.

(Photo credit Bryan Bedder/Getty)

(Photo credit Larry Busacca/Getty)

POSING WITH BEYONCÉ
BACKSTAGE AT THE GRAMMY AWARDS.

◄••••••••••

••••••••••►

BACKSTAGE WITH PROFESSIONAL SNOWBOARDER SHAUN WHITE AT NICKELODEON'S 23RD ANNUAL KIDS' CHOICE AWARDS.

(Photo credit Chris Polk/KCA2010/Getty)

(Photo credit Frank Micelotta/Getty)

PERFORMING AT NICKELODEON'S 23RD ANNUAL
KIDS' CHOICE AWARDS.

The album was unveiled with much hype and hoopla on March 19. Fans again lined up hours in advance for the chance to be one of the first to buy it. Copies were flying out of the stores. Insiders were not surprised. It would have been a colossal disappointment if the CD had not been successful. Once the dust settled, it became evident that the album was a smash-hit.

My World 2.0 debuted at 1 on the *Billboard* charts, selling 283,000 copies in its first week. That mark made Justin the youngest solo male act to top the charts since 1963, when a twelve-year-old Stevie Wonder accomplished the feat. When the album sold more copies in its second week than it did in the first, it made Justin the first artist since the Beatles to debut at number 1 and then sell more copies the following week.

Like before, reviews were mixed, but the overwhelming majority seemed to get what Justin was all about.

People magazine said that the album was a combination of "yummy rhythm-and-blues-flavored pop and a sweet soulful voice." *US* magazine said the album offered "hard to resist rhythm-and-blues-flavored pop and uniquely grown-up vocal trills." *Entertainment Weekly* praised Bieber's "rhythm-and-blues swagger which reminded [the writer] of the early days of Usher and Justin Timberlake."

Needless to say, everybody connected with Def Jam was thrilled at how quickly and how well the album had performed. The record label's head honcho, L.A. Reid,

had long championed Justin and would take every opportunity to praise his client. In a press release from the time
of *My World 2.0*'s release, Reid exclaimed, "Justin is nothing short of a phenomenon. It's so rare to find any artist
this young with such pure star quality, such a dynamic
presence, and such musical gifts."

Justin wanted to celebrate the release of *My World 2.0*,
and rather than have the typical music industry party, he
preferred to have some old-fashioned fun. Strings were
pulled and soon Justin and a close circle of friends were
celebrating at the Lucky Strike Lanes bowling alley in
New York City. Things were going along fine until the
inevitable crowd of fans showed up and overran the bowling alley. Everything was still more or less under control,
but Justin's security, having gone through the chaos of a
Justin appearance too many times to count, decided to
pull the plug on the event early.

Justin had always stated that all he wanted was to be a
regular kid. But on nights like this, he knew those days
were gone forever.

Justin continued to be active through the remainder of
March, appearing in concert at a Houston rodeo with
Selena Gomez. Despite the already strong support for Justin in Texas, there was some question as to how young
fans in a state known for being conservative would react
to the flash of his performance. There was no reason to
worry. As soon as Justin swaggered onstage, waved to the
crowd, and started to sing, the power of his performance

instantly cut through any preconceived notions. Justin had easily taken Houston.

In a surprising bit of irony, Justin accepted an invitation to perform at *American Idol*'s annual charity show, Idol Gives Back—the irony being that he had now reached the age when he could have auditioned to be on the show. But he did not have to because his career had exceeded even the wildest dreams of *American Idol* contestants.

Justin also discovered that he was now a media darling at a major-league level. Top network shows, including ABC's *Nightline* and *CBS Evening News,* featured lengthy interview segments with him. It was amusing to watch veteran journalists such as Katie Couric, who were more familiar with interviewing politicians and European royalty, try in vain to approach Justin from a fresh angle or ask a probing question. Although fun to watch, it was largely a futile effort because the story had long been out there, and the likes of *Tiger Beat, Bop,* and *Teen Vogue* had covered it pretty well.

The View was particularly captivated by Justin, so much so that they had him on two back-to-back shows. Viewers could watch the all-women panel laugh their way through asking the typical teen-fan kind of questions. It might have been a tad condescending but Justin didn't mind. Although he was young, he knew the score. *The View* was a show that was hurting in the ratings and figured that Justin's appearances would goose said ratings for a couple of days. Barbara Walters was an old pro and knew the score. She would not say it publicly but she needed Justin more than Justin needed *The View.*

Elsewhere, there was some serious talking going on. Justin had already shown his ability on the concert stage countless times. The people guiding his career felt it was time for him to take the next step, which meant a mammoth headlining tour. It was easier said than done. A lot went into putting together that kind of tour. So while Justin continued on as before, the ins and outs of his concert tour debut were in motion.

And then there were those driving lessons.

It was something that had been kept under wraps. But sometime before turning sixteen, Justin began pestering his parents, as well as every adult in his entourage, to teach him how to drive. At first, his request was laughed off, but eventually he had to be taken seriously. Pattie did not have the stomach for the task and so the job of teaching Justin how to drive fell to his father, Jeremy.

As Justin's new life dictated, Jeremy would occasionally go on the road with his son. An already close relationship was made even closer as Jeremy got to experience firsthand the excitement surrounding his son's celebrity. When it was suggested that Jeremy should be the one to teach Justin to drive, he was all for it. On those rare occasions when there was some down time on the road, or when Justin could slip back to Canada for a day or two, Jeremy and Justin would find a secluded spot and Justin would get behind the wheel.

How those driving lessons went have been kept secret but what is known is that Jeremy is a patient man and Justin, while anxious, took the lessons seriously. What is also known is that by the time Usher presented Justin with the Range Rover, Justin was reportedly more than capable of driving it. Now only one thing remained.

Finding the time to take his driver's test.

15. THE MANY LOVES OF JUSTIN BIEBER

Does Justin have a girlfriend? We may now have the evidence.

Shortly before he turned sixteen, Justin was at an event. The fans were screaming. The crowd was intense. The paparazzi's cameras were going off like fireworks. That's when a camera man from TMZ caught the images. Justin walking through the crowd . . . with a girl on his arm! She was walking close. Slightly taller than Justin. Long, shoulder-length hair. Cute. And it was clear that she only had eyes for Justin.

Her name was never disclosed. And apparently the pair were taking great pains to avoid the secret getting out because, to date, no other pictures of Justin and the mystery girl have surfaced. But then, there have been rumors of Justin dating ever since he moved to Atlanta, so this was nothing new. However, this latest sighting only served to fan the flames of an ongoing question.

Was Justin truly in a relationship? Was he in love?

"I haven't been in love yet but I've felt love," he said in a 2009 interview with *M Magazine.* "It's a beautiful emotion that you can't really describe."

Defending the notion of a youngster singing songs about love when he hasn't really experienced the emotion, he told the *Sun,* "No matter what age you are, you still know love. I haven't been in love but I do love girls."

Whatever the case, Justin has shown a definite interest in the ladies, almost from the day he was born. Since coming to prominence, Justin has made a point of saying in several interviews that he has always felt love for his mother, Pattie. Which is an innocent kind of affection that is not out of the ordinary. And perhaps, because of his relationship with his mother, as he has come to be interested in girls romantically, he has created an image of an ideal girl based very much upon his mother's best traits. And since an important part of the *Tiger Beat* style of preteen-oriented journalism is to ask a celebrity to describe his ideal girl, Justin has laid out a fairly basic answer.

In a recent interview with radio station WWWQ, Justin explained, "A girl has to have nice eyes, a nice smile, and be a girl that can make me laugh." In an interview that appeared on the Angry Ape Web site, he furthered that description: "I look for a pretty girl who is nice, laid-back, and funny."

Justin's mother acknowledged in a *J-14* interview that the perfect girlfriend for Justin would be someone "who has similar values and keeps him grounded."

With his boyish good looks, constant smile, and loving nature toward his fans, he has become the ideal for millions of teenage girls. When they chase him down the street or grab at him at his personal appearances, it can't be anything but a feeling of love. Justin told TheStar.com that the feeling was mutual. "Girl fans are great," he explained. "They always show up with hats and gifts and I always thank them. I wouldn't be where I am right now if it wasn't for their support."

Given his age and popularity, one would almost expect the teen to take advantage of his status by seeking physical relationships with his fans. However, Justin, at least at this point, is chaste in his approach to romance. He has often said that he is shy about approaching girls and maintains that he will remain a virgin until he gets married.

But Justin's attitude toward love and girls has definitely gone through a few changes as his career has blossomed, mainly because aside from concerts and public appearances, he is primarily around adults. And the ease with which he functions in adult situations, mixed with the level of celebrity he has attained, has given him, at an age when most boys have a healthy interest in girls anyway, a sense of bravado and ego when it comes to being around the opposite sex.

This quickly became evident during his early appearances on radio and television talk shows. If an interviewer was female and struck his fancy, he was quick to ask whether she had a boyfriend and if she wanted to go on a date. The hosts would always laugh at his preteen attempts at flirting.

A perfect example of this assuredness came in an interview on MTV when Justin was asked who he felt was his dream date. "I can pick any girl I want," he said with no small sense of ego. "I'm gonna take Meagan Good, Kim Kardashian, Megan Fox. Whoever I fall in love with. It can be anybody."

Of any celebrity status or any age.

During a recent appearance at the White House, Justin mixed and mingled with President Obama and his family. However, as he related in an interview that appeared on the Angry Ape Web site, he was paying particular attention to the President's wife, Michelle. "I told her she was very beautiful and that she had nice legs."

At one point in 2009, a supposed relationship with dancer Jaquelle came and went. A bit higher up the romance rumor line was that Justin was seeing actress Elissa Sursara on a regular basis. That report actually began gathering so much steam that a spokesperson for Justin had to step in and set the record straight, and state that Justin had asked for the girl's phone number and that she politely declined, saying she only wanted to be friends.

Easily his most overt flirtation has been with superstar performer Beyoncé. He has remarked on several occasions that he has been in love with Beyoncé since he was seven years old. And the feeling only intensified years later when their paths would cross at business and social functions.

The first was a 2009 get-together backstage at the Grammys, where they exchanged pleasantries and hugged. She gave him a peck on the cheek. Justin recalled what happened next. "I told her she was good-looking. Actually, she was hot."

And she was also very married to rap/hip-hop impresario Jay-Z, who was close enough to hear Justin's comments. But Jay-Z took it the right way, pretending to be offended and joking that this young boy would hit on his wife right in front of him. He knew it was a mild teenage crush and nothing more. However, to this day, Justin does not see it that way.

In comments in *Star* and *Details,* Justin elaborated on his feelings for the hip-hop superstar.

"She kind of broke my heart when she married Jay-Z," he said. "I actually had butterflies in my stomach when I met her. I really had a crush on her and wanted to date her. I'm just waiting for her to call. She's my ideal woman."

But while he's waiting, Justin has continued to flirt with other—and yes, older—women. His most recent highly publicized adventure came when he was part of the all-star lineup singing the remake of "We Are the World," and came face to face with Nicole Scherzinger, the beautiful,

talented, and very much in a relationship member of the
Pussycat Dolls. Nicole recalled in detail, in an article that
appeared on the Angry Ape Web site, what happened the
night Justin walked into the recording studio.

"I was in the recording studio, talking to Lionel Richie
and Toni Braxton," she remembered. "There were a whole
bunch of other people in the room. All of a sudden Justin
walks in. He sits back, puts his hands on his hips, looks at
me, and goes, 'I can't take it. I gotta leave. You're just too
gorgeous.' And then he just walked out."

Justin gave his side of that encounter during an interview with *E!* "When we recorded the Haiti charity song,
I was singing my part to Nicole. It was hard to take my
eyes off her because she's so gorgeous."

Consequently the press has had a field day, generating
rumors on an almost everyday basis about who Justin has
a crush on or who he would like to date. Justin has often
commented on some of the speculation and has laughed
at some of the more outrageous theories of who is hot in
his eyes.

When Kim Kardashian suggested that her younger
sister, Kelly, might be the perfect date for Justin, he dismissed that notion but quickly said that he would like to
date Kim. And shortly after his 2010 appearance on *Saturday Night Live,* he made no bones about the fact that he
would be interested in dating Tina Fey.

While it may appear that Justin is not too particular
when it comes to the opposite sex, he definitely has

standards, and there are certain lines he will not cross. Yes, love is important but so is friendship.

He has often dismissed the notion that he and Taylor Swift had long ago hooked up, insisting that they are very good friends and nothing more. He has said that Miley Cyrus is not his type and that he has no interest in Selena Gomez, despite her being very pretty.

But Rihanna? Justin is definitely interested.

On an appearance on *The Ellen DeGeneres Show,* he recounted how he had met Rihanna at the Grammys and she had kissed him on the cheek. For Justin, that was the opening he was looking for. He immediately asked her out on a date. She turned him down. The audience gave him sympathetic support. Justin was not upset by the rejection. He smiled and said, "Maybe in a few years."

16. Leave It To Bieber

It was March 16. As he spoke into the multitude of microphones, and photographer's flashes went off all around him, Justin announced that he was going on tour for the first time. And it was going to be a monster of an experience.

His first headlining North American tour, the My World tour, would begin on June 23 in Hartford, Connecticut, trek through forty cities, and end in Allentown, Pennsylvania, on September 4. Justin enthusiastically told the press that there would be a big stage setup, a terrific sound system, and, above all, "a place where you can expect to have a great time and to, hopefully, be able to relate to the songs."

Tickets went on sale for Justin's tour a week later and,

according to reports, a week later almost all the shows on the tour had sold out. An unbelievable feat in light of the tight economic times. But for the fans buying up tickets in bunches, the expense was worth it to see their idol live, up close and personal.

However, there was much to do and many miles to log before Justin took to the road.

Justin continued hitting the late-night talk-show circuit, being cute and clever with both David Letterman and Jay Leno. On Leno's show, it was becoming evident that Justin was somewhat out of sorts. He looked tired and his responses were a little on the scattered and mechanical side. More than one person was thinking that Justin could use a few days off.

Justin had always been respectful to everyone he met and could never be accused of being arrogant. But it was during the Jay Leno appearance that Justin showed a very rare moment of impatience when a cameraman did something he did not like, and he shouted out "That's dumb" loud enough for everybody to hear. Immediately one of his security people took Justin aside and told him to calm down.

Justin's growing confidence and, yes, no small amount of ego, created some stir around this time when he basically dissed both Disney and Nickelodeon for the "corny" way in which they manufactured pop stars like Miley Cyrus and that people like himself, Justin Timberlake, and Usher had made it without going that route. It was controversial to say the least but it was also true so who could argue with him. Certainly not Disney or Nickelodeon who never responded to Justin's comments.

His initial meeting with President Obama, for the *Christmas in Washington* special, had gone so well that the President and First Lady invited him back to the White House for the annual Easter Egg Roll on April 5.

The event, held on the White House lawn, was attended by *Harry Potter* author J. K. Rowling, actress Reese Witherspoon, and the cast of the television series *Glee,* among others. Still, considerable attention was paid to Justin, who was perhaps using this opportunity to give the more than 30,000 people at the event an idea of what his upcoming tour would be like.

Justin took the stage with a full backup band and complement of backup singers. From his own song list he did "One Time," "Baby," and "U Smile" before bringing down the house with a medley that included Michael Jackson's "Wanna Be Starting Somethin'" and the Aerosmith/Run-DMC version of "Walk This Way."

With the performance over, Justin got to play tourist in a very big way. He spent time with the President's daughters and took pictures with the First Family. "I got to hang out with the President in the Oval Office, which was crazy," he recalled in an article that appeared on DailyFill .com, "because no one really gets to go in there. But it was pretty incredible."

As was the announcement, made shortly before the

White House visit, that Justin would be the musical guest on the April 10 episode of *Saturday Night Live*. What may have seemed a spur of the moment decision to have Justin on the show, was in fact the result of behind-the-scenes negotiations that had been going on for a year.

Originally he was simply going to sing a song or two during the show. But the SNL writers immediately latched onto the idea of playing with Justin's status as a teenage pop star. It was a bit of a gamble for Justin. To what degree would his making light of his own persona effect his hardcore fans, who took their feelings and loyalty to Justin very seriously? But Justin was up to the challenge and so things went forward, with much of the comedic bits involving him and host Tina Fey.

There were concerns that Justin might be setting himself up for a fall. But in an interview with the *Sun*, Justin dismissed them. "I'm not afraid of looking stupid," he said matter-of-factly.

In the show's opening monologue, Justin stood bemused as Fey cracked a couple of jokes about the large number of young girls in the audience and Justin's position as a role model. Later in the show, Justin and Fey did a brief comic duet on the song "I'm Every Woman." The show's high point had Justin playing a high school student in a class taught by Fey. In the sketch, Fey's character had the hots for Justin, who flirted with her and sang a medley of fantasy songs to get her temperature rising. During the musical portion of the show, Justin drove the audience wild with "Baby" and "U Smile."

Justin scored major points with SNL's staff, who considered him a pro. The show's executive producer, Lorne Michaels, related that when they had to change elements of his sketch mere moments before airtime, he immediately picked up on them and hit his marks well. Afterward, Justin told the press that the experience was "hilarious and a lot of fun to do."

But the experience paled in comparison to the most important event that could possibly take place in a young man's life. On April 13, Justin and his mother slipped into an Atlanta Department of Motor Vehicles office and he successfully completed the necessary tests to become a licensed driver. He had tried to keep the event private but with paparazzi stalking his every move, images of Justin walking through the DMV office and posing for a series of license photos quickly became front-page Internet news all over the world. It was reported in several news outlets that Justin immediately jumped into the Range Rover that Usher had given him and took his first solo drive. Reportedly, the first things Justin did were pick up his friends and go out for something to eat.

"I couldn't wait to get my license," he told *J-14*. "I was excited at the freedom and responsibility that comes with it."

There would be little time to break in his new driving

privileges as he was soon off on yet another round-the-world jaunt. It would begin in Canada where he was a sure bet among industry insiders to walk away with several awards on the April 18 Juno Awards show.

Justin was in full-on country pride mode as his plane touched down in the town of St. Johns, just outside of Newfoundland, where the awards were being held. When it came time for him to walk down the red carpet, Justin was escorted by two uniformed Royal Canadian Mounties. During the show, Justin again played up Canada during a performance of his hit "Baby." Ludacris was not around to do the song's rap but the crowd went wild when fellow Canuck and good buddy Drake sauntered on stage to do the bit. Later, Justin joined others in a rendition of the K'naan song "Wavin' Flag."

But the rest of the evening would be considered a major disappointment to industry insiders, when Justin failed to pick up any of the awards he had been nominated for. However, he seemed unphased by the slight. Just being in his home country and paying tribute to the talent around him was more than enough award for him. Besides, there really was not enough time to contemplate what many considered to be his first career downer.

Justin was now scheduled to begin an odyssey that would take him first to Japan and then to Australia. But Mother Nature had different plans. The eruption of a volcano in Iceland was having worldwide repercussions, with ash causing international flight delays and cancellations. Undeterred,

Justin and his entourage managed to get a flight from St. Johns to Toronto, where they took advantage of a window of opportunity and were soon flying east.

As he boarded the plane for Japan, Justin tweeted his fans on what he would be doing. "Gearing up for an eighteen-hour flight to Tokyo. Going to sleep and see every movie that I haven't seen for the past two years."

Japan was going to be a new experience for Justin. He had never been there before but he already knew that Japanese fans loved his music. But what kind of reception would he receive once his plane touched down at Narita Airport in Tokyo was anybody's guess.

Justin need not have been worried. Girls screaming and holding up handwritten signs greeted him as he stepped off the plane. Pictures of him were everywhere. He could immediately sense that he was going to like Japan.

He spent the next few days in and around Tokyo, doing a lengthy round of press interviews and radio appearances. An interpreter was on hand to translate Japanese to English and vice versa, but although the language barrier was there, the questions remained the same. Talking about his love life in Japan was pretty much the same as talking about his love life every other place he'd been.

This being Japan, he could not pass up the opportunity to do a little sightseeing and so, in every spare moment, he was on the streets, sampling the native food, looking at historical landmarks, and meeting the people. Unlike the crowd that greeted him at the airport, people he encountered on the street were mostly reserved and polite, and they were always friendly. On those occasions, Justin was grateful for even the smallest break in the nonstop hysteria that followed him. Japan proved a momentary port in the storm; Australia would be his next stop.

For the most part, the flight to Australia was uneventful. An unexpected highlight for the music-savvy Justin was the presence of rock guitarist Slash on the flight, and the two enjoyed talking shop at 30,000 feet.

The hysteria that greeted Justin when the plane landed was not a surprise. After getting through the crowd, he spent a good part of the day playing football on a popular Sydney beach until the appearance of fans and paparazzi made his security team uneasy and he was quickly whisked away amid screams of "Justin! I love you!" However, before he left, Justin did his good deed for the day when a girl came up to him and shyly announced that it was her birthday. Justin instantly broke into a rendition of "Happy Birthday" for the astonished girl and her friends before security finally said enough was enough.

It was during his beach frolic that a long-held secret was finally revealed. One of the rash of paparazzi hounding Justin's every move managed to get a shot of him without his shirt, and the photo clearly showed what appeared to be a small tattoo of a bird on his hip. Speculation that Justin had gotten himself inked ran rampant for days. Some suggested that it had to be a temporary tattoo. Others were convinced that it was real.

Justin eventually confirmed that the tattoo was indeed real and that it was part of a family tradition to get one.

A big part of the attraction on the trip to Sydney was to give Justin's fans an opportunity to see him perform live the next day at an outdoor location near a shopping center. The three-song set was scheduled to begin at 7:40 AM on April 25. Not surprisingly, thousands of teenage girls began arriving at the location twenty-four hours in advance. There was some tension in the air but, for the most part, things appeared fairly calm by Justin Bieber appearance standards.

Until 2 AM Monday morning, when all hell broke loose.

According to reports filed initially by the *New Zealand Herald* and later picked up by *USA Today,* the *Los Angeles Times,* and others, a rumor began circulating that Justin had arrived early and was in the area. The fuse was lit. For the next few hours, the crowds began surging forward and crushing others in an attempt to get closer to where their idol supposedly was. Some fans were reportedly trampled and many received injuries. As a result, a total of eight had to be transported to a nearby hospital, and many in the crowd suffered from hyperventilation. After witnessing this, the local police force officially canceled the performance before it started. For some hours afterward, there would be reports of thousands of disappointed teenage girls milling around the streets.

Justin was awake and ready to go to the location to do

the show when he received word that the police had canceled it. Not wanting a repeat of what had happened in Long Island, he immediately put out a Twitter message to his fans, explaining what had happened and apologizing. In an attempt to make up for the cancellation, Justin's people hastily arranged a one-song performance later that same day behind a glass window in front of Channel Seven Studios, where Justin would be doing press and appearing on the *Sunrise Show.* Justin performed "Baby" to a screaming crowd on April 25 and, at the end of the segment, promised to return to Sydney in the not too distant future with a full-scale concert.

The crowd continued to mill around outside the studio; many were upset at the brevity of the performance and the fact that Justin chose to sing behind a glass partition. There was still a lot of tension in the air, made all the more tense by an announcement from the police for the crowd to disperse. For his part, Justin attempted to calm things down when he told the crowd, "I guess police say that you guys have to go home. I'd love for you guys to stay and hang out, but we've got to go."

In the aftermath of Justin's Australian appearance, the consensus was that the chaos did not come as a surprise and that local law enforcement should have known better and prepared accordingly.

The next stop on the tour was Auckland, New Zealand. The authorities there said that what happened in Sydney would not be allowed to recur. Well in advance of the already-growing hysteria surrounding Justin's upcoming appearance, authorities warned that security measures would be enhanced and that there would be the tightest control possible.

So when the plane carrying Justin landed in Auckland, in the middle of the night, the estimated 500 screaming fans were kept in check by a large number of local police. The atmosphere was more subdued, and all the elements of a Justin Bieber personal appearance were in place.

Until things again got out of hand. Some fans persisted in testing the security wall around Justin and eventually broke through. One girl grabbed the hat off Justin's head and ran out of the airport. Another wave of young girls slammed into Justin's mother and knocked her to the ground. Eventually Pattie and Justin were able to reach the nearby SUV and were driven to safety.

Over the next few hours, the New Zealand assault became big international news when the young girl who took the hat said she would return it to Justin if he gave her a hug. Justin was upset and, despite the fact that his mother immediately texted fans, "Thanks for all your support. I'm okay," Justin tweeted his fans that he was *not* pleased.

"I'm grateful that everyone is excited," he said. "But I'm not happy that a fan stole my hat and that my mom was knocked down. If you're a fan, just show me the respect that I try and show you."

Justin's New Zealand stopover was to include a

meet-and-greet with his fans. But given the incident at the airport, it was immediately cancelled. Now that there was a little time to kill, Justin decided to have some fun. With his entourage nervously trailing behind, Justin went to the Auckland Harbor Bridge and bungee-jumped off of it. His mother and security people heaved a sigh of relief when the bungee cord did not snap. But then Pattie got into the spirit of the moment when she and a member of the security team made jumps of their own. Not surprisingly, Justin filmed the jump and footage immediately made its way onto the Internet.

Justin was so excited after the jump that he said that he wanted to try skydiving next. Everybody in Justin's entourage said a silent prayer that they would be able to talk him out of that little adventure.

Despite the chaos, Justin made good on his promise to do a free mini-concert for 500 students at the Strathalan High School For Girls. His six-song set for the enthusiastic fans also included a rare moment of Justin getting behind a drum set and showing off his percussion skills.

Shortly before Justin left New Zealand, the girl who stole the hat called and arranged a meeting to formally return it. The meeting, according to eyewitnesses, was tense. Justin got his hat back. But the girl did not get her hug. Shortly after the exchange, Justin texted his fans: "I'm just glad they did the right thing. I don't condone thievery."

Around the time of his New Zealand adventure, the

single "Somebody to Love" was released. A straightforward, danceable tune, the single probably would have been successful but, as had been the case with other cuts from the same album, not an international hit had it not been for an unexpected Usher tie-in. It was known that Usher had sung backing vocals on the track. What was made public around the time of its release was that the track had originally been slated to be on an Usher album. It is unclear why Usher passed on the song, but Justin was definitely the beneficiary.

Reviews of the song were positive but subdued. The *Boston Herald* called it "fun and upbeat." The *National Post* said it "sounds like Timbaland." *BBC Music* stated that the song was "a straightforward plea for a soul mate."

There was already a lot on Justin's plate. But if even half of the rumors floating around by the end of April were true, Justin was going to have to start taking more naps. The latest speculation was that he was being sought for a song on the soundtrack of the third *Twilight* movie, *Eclipse*. There was also chatter that the queen of talk shows, Oprah Winfrey, was eager to get the young star on her show.

What turned out to be true was the announcement that Justin would make a second trip to *The Today Show*, in the middle of preparations for his first headlining tour, for a June 4 appearance as part of *Today*'s Summer Concert Series.

While he would continue to make some promotional appearances in the coming weeks, much of his time was now spent in rehearsals with his band and backup dancers; preparing for the start of the tour, on June 23. There were song lists to finalize, choreography to fine-tune—in other words, the basic lights/camera/action that would be part of the ultimate Justin Bieber experience.

Justin dropped hints of things to come during an interview with the *Houston Chronicle*. "I want to show that I love to perform. There's going to be some cool tricks and some electronic things that haven't been seen before."

Word of Justin's tour had spread like wildfire. It seemed like every young girl on the planet was moving heaven and earth to get a ticket. Shows were selling out in a matter of days and there were already rumors that the tour might be extended to include extra shows.

Adding to the hype surrounding Justin was a comment made by Usher in an article that appeared on the Aceshowbiz site. Usher boasted that his singer was just like the Beatles were at the beginning. "You haven't seen the best of him yet," he enthused. "Justin reminds me of myself at that age. Only he's a much more talented musician than I was."

Justin was appreciative of the praise. However, he was aware that it was a lot to live up to.

Behind the scenes, schedules were being finalized and venues were being contacted. Initially the My World tour was going to be strictly a U.S. round of shows. But now there was talk of maybe hopping over to Europe and possibly going back to Asia.

Many people knew what Justin could deliver in a live performance but just as many were taking a wait-and-see attitude. Given all the hype surrounding the tour, "good" was not going to be good enough.

Justin would have to be great.

17. THE MORE THINGS CHANGE

It was bound to happen. It was not uncommon among young pop singers. In the past many singers had seen their careers come to a crashing halt because of it. And there was nothing anybody could do about it.

Justin's voice was changing.

The cracks and pitch changes are all a part of puberty. It was something that came to Justin gradually. Initially it was his speaking voice that would crack or pop at a strange level. It always brought a good-natured laugh but, in most people's eyes, could be dismissed as a cold or sore throat. Some knew Justin's voice was ripe for change but chose to ignore it.

Justin began to notice his voice changing around the time he turned sixteen. However, his fans had apparently remained unaware, and the reason for that was simple. When Justin had been singing live, all anyone could hear were the screams of young girls, which, to a very large extent, drowned out his vocals. There were also occasional sound-system glitches that helped mask the reality of his singing.

Nevertheless, Justin knew. He was straining on higher notes and octaves and he could sense that he was often not pitch perfect all the way through a song. Justin being Justin, though, he didn't think twice about spilling the beans in April when he went public with the situation to a slew of news outlets.

"I've been struggling to sing some of my songs because my voice is now cracking," he revealed. "It cracks like every teenage boy. I can't hit some of the notes I hit on 'Baby' anymore. I've been working with a vocal coach and we've lowered the key on some of the songs."

Outwardly, Justin felt he could overcome the vocal changes and radiated good humor and confidence when asked about the change. But when he said that he only thought positively about the situation, one could sense that the singer was hoping for the best and was, perhaps, having some doubts. Justin was reassured by his management and label people that a voice change was not an uncommon situation for a singer and there would be no problem in modifying the songs to fit the change. Although nobody was saying so publicly, there was already much speculation that future songs would be structured to work within

Justin's evolving vocal range. It was a fact of life that was to be met and dealt with.

Justin would get a chance to showcase his revamped singing range before he hit the road. In mid-April he accepted an offer to be a part of the annual day-long concert event Wango Tango, scheduled for May 15. He would be in good company; the lineup included such pop luminaries as Usher, Adam Lambert, Ludacris, Ke$ha, Akon, and others. Justin had always been a team player and he made it plain that he felt honored to be performing in that kind of company. But as the date of the event drew closer, it became evident by the promos for the show and the speed in which the tickets sold once Justin was announced, that Justin was a driving force in the event.

Justin was not being shown any favoritism in being selected for the show but, although unspoken, there was always the question of how more established and, yes, older performers would react to a much younger singer getting the lion's share of the spotlight. Happily, everybody Justin had come in contact with was secure in their own status and would often be generous in sharing their experiences and advice with him.

With fame had come a slew of honors from different magazines and TV shows. In Justin's case, it was a given that he would be the darling of the teen magaines and make the ten-best list in any number of categories. Sexiest? Most Handsome? The Person You'd Most Like to Share a Cab With? You name it. Justin was on that list.

Around the same time, Justin did his customary aw-shucks routine when he was notified that he had been selected for *People* magazine's annual "Most Beautiful People" list. That kind of honor was fun and it reflected his popularity, especially with the ladies, and, as he had been advised, any publicity was good publicity. But he had already matured to the point that it did not mean much in the overall scheme of things. What remained important was pleasing his fans and making good music.

Rumors continued to swirl around Justin through the month of April. The most outrageous was the report that he had decided he just wanted to be a regular kid again and that he would attend Thousand Oaks High School in Thousand Oaks, California, as a full-time student in the fall. The reason for this was that it would allow him to play high school sports. Representatives from the school, who suddenly found themselves dealing with worldwide media attention, claimed they had heard the rumor but could not confirm or deny anything, which only served the give the story additional life. Behind the scenes, Justin's entourage must have laughed at the youthful enthusiasm that led Justin to make that announcement.

Because, to their way of thinking, there was no way that scenario was going to happen.

For better or worse, Justin's life and career had moved well beyond the point where he could go to a public high school and act like a "regular" student. He would be an ongoing distraction to the school and the rest of the students and teachers. Security would be a constant presence. The school would be constantly under siege by the press and fanatical young girls. The dream could very easily become a nightmare.

Justin seemed to sense the absurdity of attending a public high school or doing just about anything he used to do by the time he sat down with an Associated Press reporter in May and reflected on the fact that perhaps "regular" might be a bit out of reach at this point.

He agreed that one of his idols, the late Michael Jackson, had lost all semblance of normalcy in his life at a very early age, but, as he acknowledged, "At least I had my childhood from age one to thirteen."

"People always ask me, 'Do you wish you had a regular life?' And I'm, like, 'You know, not really.' Sometimes I want to be just regular, just hanging out or whatever. There's ups and downs to everything."

In the same interview he explained that even the initial idea of flying his friends out to wherever he happens to be for a weekend, just to hang out, has, in the past year, butted up against the reality of stardom. If it's not a day specifically set aside for Justin to do nothing, the friend will often be hanging out in the hotel or tagging along with Justin while he conducts business. Days for doing things like shooting hoops and playing video games often fall by the wayside despite the best efforts of his management and family to give him the time off.

Justin admitted that it is not always easy to hang out

when he wants to. "I try to spend as much time with my friends and just be as regular a kid as I can on top of work," he said.

Despite the chaos that ensued the last time he visited Paris, Justin insisted on making another trip to the City of Lights for a quick promotional stop. He knew what to expect and he got it in spades.

Hysterical girls following him everywhere he went. Paparazzi trailing behind him and getting in his way. Normally Justin would not let the shutterbugs get to him and, truth be known, he found the press attention a lot of fun and something he instinctively gravitated toward.

But something may have happened this time to set him off.

On a quick stop in at a Paris McDonalds, he was chatting up a pretty young French girl who had stepped from the crowd and boldly engaged him in conversation. There was a smile on his face that would not go away. For the moment, Justin was simply a normal kid engaging in a perfectly normal teenage flirtation.

According to reports from TMZ, the pair ended up leaving the restaurant together. Whether anything came of the meeting was anybody's guess but it was noted that sometime later Justin and his entourage, minus the girl, were seen pushing rather roughly through a throng of photographers, with Justin reportedly doing some very angry pushing all his own. Had the intrusion of celebrity gotten in the way of Justin hooking up? Nobody would say for sure.

It was noticed that now Justin would occasionally get outwardly uptight at the celebrity photographers' intrusions. He understood that this was a part of the burden of stardom and, hey, they were only doing their job. But it did not mean that he always had to like it. Perhaps he even fantasized about going somewhere where there were no paparazzi.

Justin was inclined to stay on a pretty even keel emotionally. You'd have a hard time finding anyone who claimed to have seen Justin lose his temper. No matter how tired he was, he always seemed to have a smile and a good word for anybody who approached him. If anybody knew differently, his parents probably would, but in countless interviews Pattie had insisted that Justin, despite the mischievous moments and the odd bit of acting out, was a happy kid who was basking in the success and having the time of his life.

Oprah Winfrey's persistence paid off when Justin agreed that it would be a perfect send-off for his summer tour to appear on her show. In typical *Oprah* fashion, the search went out for an audience that would be made up of the ultimate Justin fans, which would make for excitement and good television. For Oprah, the Justin circus had definitely come to town. She knew the level of interest he generated would translate into viewers and ratings. She had to have him, and she finally did.

In preparation for his upcoming tour, Justin was also making occasional live appearances, more as a way to fine-tune his performing skills for the tour than to promote his two albums (which had sold millions of copies to date and really did not need the additional push). This is why, with only two weeks before the tour was set to begin, he agreed to appear at the Atlantis Paradise Island Resort in the Bahamas on June 12. At first glance, this show seemed a bit tricky.

It was essentially a private concert for well-to-do resort guests only. It would offer an opportunity for Justin to unwind a bit and hang out at the beach. But for the people who made a living thinking about such things, there was some cause for concern. Justin was running the risk of being typecast as just another Las Vegas lounge performer, an often true image of performers past their commercial prime, who were settling for easy gigs and big money. But management thought it was a good move and Justin responded with a solid concert performance that gave hints of what would come in the summer.

Justin's familiarity with President Obama made it natural for him to return to Washington for the annual White House Correspondents dinner, at which the President lets down his hair and cracks jokes at his own expense, and the expense of others. Young Hollywood was very much represented at the event. Managers and publicists were calling in every possible favor to get a coveted ticket for their clients.

Of particular interest was the presence of the Jonas Brothers, whom many had predicted would be overtaken in the preteen popularity contest by Justin. There had long been rumors of a feud that had been fueled by some off-the-cuff remarks made by Justin and Nick Jonas. The comments were said in jest but taken by the public as evidence of hostility between the teen pop stars. For Justin the idea of a pop star feud was dumb and not to be taken seriously.

However, what Justin discovered was that feuds between stars are a big part of how pop-star journalism works. Yes, there was the sweetness and light of *Tiger Beat*–style questions. But eventually that became old and, in order to sell magazines, or generate Web site hits, there had to be some controversy. And what better way to increase interest than to start a rivalry, whether imagined or not?

Justin laughed out loud when President Obama cracked a joke about the Jonas Brothers' interest in his daughters, and the big guns he could bring to bear. That Justin maintained a rather low profile at the proceedings, and was spared being the butt of any jokes, was fine with him. He was only there to hang out and have a good time. And to meet some people.

The next day, though, Justin tweeted his fans, saying he and Nick Jonas had been texting back and forth and had agreed that the comments they had put out on the Internet were all in fun and that there was no bad blood between them.

During the evening's after-party, Justin was the center of attention in many quarters. Veteran politicians, many old enough to have grandchildren Justin's age, were quick to introduce themselves, pose for photos, and shake his hand. Justin said a brief hello to the President and First Lady and was all smiles as he cruised through the evening as one of the night's "must meets" on a number of guests' agendas.

Justin did have a fun, if unexpected, encounter that night. He was coming out of the men's room when a very large, athletic-looking man approached him. The man literally towered over him. The man stopped, extended his hand to shake Justin's, and introduced himself as NFL superstar Donovan McNabb, the quarterback of the Washington Redskins. McNabb asked if he could take a picture with Justin. Justin readily agreed. As the two posed for the camera, McNabb jokingly said, "I've got daughters. This will help me out at home."

However, Justin's willingness to meet and greet, and have his photo taken with any number of celebrities and politicians would, in one instance, come back to haunt him.

While mixing and mingling before and after the dinner, Justin was introduced to Kim Kardashian. The reality star of the show *Keeping Up with the Kardashians* had long been on a list of Justin's fantasy loves, and when he saw her across the room, he knew he had to meet her.

There were good words between them as they posed for the paparazzi's cameras and, not unexpectedly, within hours the photos of them together went international on every possible Web site and blog. It was no big deal until Justin followed up with a tweet of his own attached to the photos in which he said that Kim was now his girlfriend.

At first, Justin's comments were taken about as seriously as any others he had made in the past about women and girls. It was innocent and did not mean a whole lot. But declaring his interest in Kardashian unexpectedly struck a nerve with his fans.

Justin's fans were incensed that this older celebrity, who, in fact, few of his fans liked or related to, had made that much of an impression on the young star. The Internet was immediately bombarded with not-too-veiled threats against Kim, which, over the course of twenty-four hours, had gotten so angry and hostile in nature that Kim tweeted Justin and asked him to do something to calm his fans down. Justin obliged and immediately tweeted his fans to say that he and Kim were just good friends and that everybody should calm down. Reportedly, that diffused the situation. But fans have remained on the alert for any serious Justin crushes that they do not approve of.

A short time after Justin's plea for sanity among his fans, Kardashian, in an interview with *US* magazine, acknowledged that she was still receiving threats but that she would not let them get in the way of her being friends with Justin. "I still have 'Bieber Fever.' It's not his fault that all his fans are after me. They're all young so I'm hoping that it's all just in fun and they aren't serious."

Unfortunately, Kardashian seemed intent on continuing to poke the fans and would not let the situation die. As part of the *US* interview, she took a series of photos, one of which featured her in a T-shirt that proudly read MRS. BEIBER. The fact that she had misspelled Bieber on the shirt was the least of her problems.

She was making fun of the desire that millions of Justin's fans had in their hearts and dreams. The threats flamed up once again and the feeling among both fans and people in the business was that Kardashian should stop her Justin antics and disappear for a while. Or at least make eyes at somebody her own age.

Those around Justin during this period were seeing a lot of growth in the young singer. That he had blossomed into a professional entertainer in every sense of the word was not in doubt. However, what they marveled at was his growing confidence away from the stage and the spotlight.

If Justin did not like a decision being made for him, he would say so. He was quicker to show his personality and emotion during any number of situations, despite the fact that he knew that the people making the decisions knew a lot more than he did and had his best interests at heart.

But, happily, those around him saw that although Justin would occasionally act out, he was mostly devoid of "attitude."

In early May, Justin went to Chicago to tape his *Oprah Winfrey Show* appearance in preparation for its May 11 airing. The visit had been publicized but great pains had been taken to keep the particulars of his arrival top secret. So when Justin's van pulled up, there were only about ten girls hanging out excitedly near the front door. A member of Justin's entourage stuck his head out of the van, surveyed the scene, and announced that Justin would not have time to meet with them. Justin was not happy. He immediately said, "I want to hang out for a while," hopped out of the van, and proceeded to sign autographs and take pictures with the small cluster of excited fans. Chances are, if he had been consulted, Justin would have agreed with his security people's concern for his safety.

But Justin was having one of those days when he was not going to take no for an answer.

Throughout his career, Justin's support staff made a point of having either a publicity person or a security type around whenever Justin was doing interviews. While he had quickly turned into a seasoned pro at doing press, there were those occasions where he would misspeak and somebody would immediately step in to elaborate on what Justin had "really" meant to say. Because of this, there were few if any missteps. And nothing had come back to haunt him.

However, nobody seemed to be able to keep Justin

from fueling the fire of controversy when it came to ragging on those who, unlike himself, had been "created" in the Nickelodeon and Disney school of Pop Star 101—in particular, his perceived biggest competitors, the Jonas Brothers and Miley Cyrus. In several interviews, he had dismissed the Disney way of making music as "corny." Despite his handlers' best efforts, and the fact that Justin had made appearances on Nickelodeon projects, he continued to ride that horse and, in an interview with *Popstar,* was firing with both barrels.

"I'm not with Nickelodeon exclusively and I might do some stuff with Disney," he told the interviewer. "But I haven't branded myself. When people sign with Disney, they basically have them. Basically they're in a contract with Disney for so many years and they can't do anything else. If I were to sign with Disney, people would start saying, 'He's a little cookie-cutter singer.' I'm not saying anything bad about the Jonas Brothers. They're good, I like what they do, and it's the same with Miley. But all of their songs are about everything being good and perfect. Being independent allows me greater freedom."

Justin seemed to take particular pride in those attacks, feeling that his independence and his success were badges of honor. It was a sure sign of ego if ever there was one.

Justin was smart enough to realize that having anything approaching a normal childhood at this point was next to impossible. But more and more, he was insisting that he needed some time off from the grind of show business.

"From the beginning, I sort of set out one day a week to be a regular kid and to do regular things," he told TheStar.com. "I don't want to be thirty and think that I didn't really do anything with my childhood."

Braun, who seemed as adept at playing a surrogate uncle or father as he was a manger, told an Associated Press interviewer pretty much the same story. "At least one day a week we do not travel, we don't do anything, we have fun," he declared. "He's a kid. We let him be a kid."

But there were indications after his appearance on *Saturday Night Live* that stardom was beginning to wear on the young singer and that his childhood was becoming a distant memory.

Reports began to surface that Justin was getting tired more easily and much more often. Whereas normally he would take one day a week off to do normal kid things, he was now spending most of his day off sleeping after the exhaustive schedule of the previous six days. It was said that Justin was now cutting his rehearsal time down to next to nothing in preparation for live performances. In response, Justin, when confronted with the reality of the grind, would only acknowledge that it was hard work but that he enjoyed it.

But he had to admit that having a career—and a much longer one than most teen idols do—was also very much on his mind. Encouraged by the success of his collaboration with Ludacris and the success of his duet with Sean Kingston, Justin was anxious to work with other people as a way of presenting an image of a real artist who was committed to having a long career and making different kinds of music.

He has told several sources, including the Web site Crushable, that he thinks the world of Taylor Swift and would love to work with her on something in the future. He also sees possibilities in a collaboration with fellow Canadian Drake. He has said on more than one occasion that if the right situation presented itself he would be thrilled to work with Kanye West and Jay-Z. Justin also made a point of informing E! Online that he would be happy to collaborate with Lil Wayne once the rapper had put his legal difficulties behind him. And it goes without saying that anytime Usher needs a hand with something, he's there.

Apparently, another long-rumored feud, between Miley Cyrus and Justin, had finally gone by the wayside as the pair were spotted early in May at a Los Angeles sushi restaurant. Pretty innocent stuff, in most people's eyes. However, the tabloids quickly proclaimed that the pair were now an item. Miley jokingly told the press that their meeting was all business and that they were actually in deep discussion about working on a side project together. With Miley's recent turn in a more adult direction, the press could only wonder what role Justin might play in her new mature world.

The so-called date with Miley continued to have legs in the tabloid press. Stories began emerging that Justin and Miley's boyfriend, Liam Hemsworth, were feuding over Miley's attention and, allegedly, there was bad blood growing between the two. Shortly after being spotted out and about with Miley, Justin paid a third visit to *The Ellen DeGeneres Show*. After the predictable questions about his fans and his hair, Ellen jumped right into the Miley dating rumor.

Justin had expected it. He indicated that he and Miley were just hanging out together. He took his response a step further and said that he hangs out with a lot of girls and that if people wanted to do a bit of research, they would know who he was talking about. For millions of young girls around the world, that comment just deepened the mystery and the fantasy.

Of course, the possibility of working with Beyoncé has never been far from Justin's mind. "I'd love to work with Beyoncé," he told the *Houston Chronicle*. "She has a great voice and is an excellent performer."

But Justin was not blind to what had gotten him to this point and so, while he made grand plans to take his music in different directions, he was quick to tell the magazine *Complex* that working with others does not necessarily mean he will deviate from the musical style that got him to the top.

"I'm trying to do my own thing at this point," he said. "It would be fun to put a little bit more rap into what I do but I think I'll keep it more pop and rhythm-and-blues."

Indeed, Justin was looking to the future and making more creative musical inroads. In early May, it was announced that he had signed a new two-record deal with Def Jam and that the first album out of that deal would most likely be recorded in New York City. Speculation instantly ran wild at the possible influence that New York's musical vibe and its new producers and songwriters might have on Justin's new music. Some quickly assumed that Justin would take a harder, hip-hop stance and that third-world elements and rap would figure heavily in any future work.

The first to publically throw his hat into the next phase of Justin's career was British pop/hip-hop singer/songwriter Taio Cruz, who acknowledged that he was in New York, talking to some producers and writing some songs. It was all kind of vague, very tantalizing, and, for Justin's legions of fans, very exciting.

Justin continued to explore other media opportunities. One of those would be the May release of "Justin Bieber Revenge," an interactive mixture of video games and music that would allow fans to experience Justin's music in a whole different way. Response to "Revenge" quickly indicated that fans wanted Justin any way they could have him.

There had been quiet concerns that Justin might be spreading himself too thin. There were also those who said Justin should strike while the iron was hot because historically the careers of teen idols were notoriously short. As always, the truth probably lay somewhere in the middle.

The Oprah Winfrey Show featuring Justin aired as scheduled, and it proved to be an entertaining, enlightening,
and emotional look at the pop star and his rise to stardom.
Justin's mother, who was also interviewed on the show,
would later tweet fans, saying the appearance brought
tears to her eyes and to those of many family members
who were in the audience. Justin performed on the show
and the consensus was that he knew appearing with Oprah
was something special, and so he gave his performance an
extra kick of energy.

The interview itself was pretty wide-ranging; he and
Oprah discussed the expected how-he-got-to-where-he-
is-now, and Justin answered such questions as how it felt
to be thought of in the company of such legendary pop
icons as Elvis Presley, Paul McCartney and, even farther
back, Frank Sinatra. Justin was also involved in an Oprah-
style "moment" when he surprised a trio of young girls
whose father, a military man, was serving in the Middle
East. He picked them up in a limo, gave them access to
a rehearsal for his *Oprah* appearance, and then presented
them with front-row seats for *Oprah* and the promise of
the best seats in the house when his national tour came to
their hometown.

Justin was in complete awe at the ease and grace with
which Oprah conducted the interview and tweeted for
days after how Oprah was a genuine woman who hung out
before and after the taping, talked to people, and acted like
a real person.

Following *Oprah*, Justin was again able to revert back to normal-boy status for a couple of hours when he was given the opportunity to throw the first pitch that night at a Chicago White Sox baseball game. Wearing a Sox jersey with his name and the number 10 on its back, Justin felt a rush of excitement as he walked out to the mound. There was surprisingly loud applause from what was considered a sports-fan base that might not know who he was. But word had traveled fast along the grapevine, and it was a good bet that some of Chicago's hardcore Bieber fans were on hand for the occasion. For the record, Justin's pitch was fairly close to the strike zone.

But like everything in show business, this high was followed closely by what would turn into an embarrassing low.

During a fairly routine recent interview with a New Zealand reporter, Justin indicated that he did not know the word "German." A video clip of this moment, illuminating Justin's alleged lack of knowledge, quickly hit the airwaves and, with so little hard news on Justin at the moment, this minor slip ridiculously became international news, with the likes of *Vanity Fair* and the prestigious *Huffington Post* taking shots at Justin for his supposed lack of education.

It was small potatoes, but Justin was more than a bit annoyed at having his intelligence bashed. He immediately hit the tweet button, and claimed the interviewer's thick accent made "German" sound like "Jewman," and that this was the cause of the confusion. But Justin was not going to stop there.

He angrily tweeted his fans a couple of days after the nonstory broke, referring to an old video in which he did indeed know his way around the country of Germany and the German language. "Old interview here in which I count in German and translate my own name [into German]. Guess I know what German is. Guess homeschooling is working out. Do your research next time before making a lame attempt at hating on a sixteen-year-old."

Right about the time the "German" issue became yesterday's news, a new nonsensical flap emerged. Justin did an interview in which he indicated he might be changing his hairstyle soon. As expected, the result was fan overkill.

Justin gets a haircut! Stop the presses!

18. THE MORE THINGS STAY THE SAME

Pop music careers rarely last very long. The music gets old. The fans move on to something else. Or more important, the fans get older. Five years is considered a great run. Three years is considered quite good. So where does Justin Bieber figure in this timeline?

May 2010. It's been approximately three years since the first time anyone heard the name Justin Bieber. Now the world cannot get through the day without hearing his name. He has been in news reports, the butt of talk-show-host jokes. If he merely woke up in Atlanta it was big news. If he woke up on the wrong side of the bed it was bigger news. The whole world had Justin on its collective mind in May 2010.

And it was proving in its coverage of Justin's life and activities that it did not take much to generate headlines.

When he snuck out to see a movie with by his body-guard, it was all over the Internet. TMZ treated the outing as an event, joking in the broadest possible sense that Justin had finally found a friend to hang out with. When it turned out that the movie he had seen was *A Nightmare on Elm Street,* the earth moved at the idea that Justin had gotten into an R-rated movie and that his handlers would allow such a thing.

Crazy Justin news was now a daily occurrence.

When he took his mother out for a day of shopping on Mother's Day in Los Angeles, in a shopping center called the Grove, he was literally leading a line of paparazzi in and out of shops and down tree-lined walkways. To the casual observer, it looked pretty funny. But to the rest of the Bieber universe, it was front-page entertainment news of the utmost importance. If it had a hint of a Justin Bieber connection, even the most commonplace incident was suddenly a very big deal. The world stopped when Justin was out and about. What was happening to Justin was what always happens when pop culture icons attain a certain level of fame. Their fans and the media pay excessive attention to things that, in the overall scheme of things, are not terribly important. For better or worse, this was now what Justin had to tolerate.

Along with the scrutiny, there were, of course, questions—questions that have been asked so many times that we know the answer before the question is even asked. Somewhere out in the big, wide journalistic world, there was a much better angle on Justin and his rise to pop stardom. But those asking the questions were too lazy to think of it. Justin did his best to put a fresh spin on things but even he had to know that there is only so much you can ask a sixteen-year-old teen idol. Nevertheless, the one question people seemingly never get tired of asking was, How did Justin Bieber take over the pop-culture world?

To be fair, Justin had already discussed this topic endless times, to the point of exhaustion. Everybody knew about the Internet videos, how he was discovered, and that he fell under the guidance of Usher. Three years in, none of this was particularly startling. So in place of the long-winded answer, Justin began answering the question in shorthand.

"Sometimes I feel like it happened fast," he told *First Look*. "But sometimes I feel like it didn't happen fast enough."

Yes, it was a sound bite. And a case could be made that it was a little bit vague. But it seemed to satisfy people.

And while his fame was skyrocketing, he maintained that members of his support system had made sure he was having as normal a childhood as possible and that maintaining that childhood was very much on their mind. In several interviews, including the one on *The Oprah Winfrey Show,* he insisted that being the biggest pop star on the planet had not gotten in the way of boundaries being set.

When not working late nights, he had a 10 PM curfew, with all Internet and Twitter activities stopping at 10:30. His mother also maintained a tough but fair hand in disciplining him. Justin offered that when he was grounded, the punishment for acting out was often the loss of his cell phone and use of the computer.

During the *Oprah* conversation, Justin sheepishly admitted that he did not get an allowance, and that for anything he wanted, he had to ask for his mother's permission. However, he acknowledged that he usually got what he asked for.

He further stood by the fact that his support system "was very small and hard to get into," but that they were dedicated to making his life as a celebrity as smooth and professionally run as possible.

Despite the hysteria, riots, and utter madness of fans that seemed to follow him wherever he goes, he continued to have nothing but good things to say about them. Even if he doesn't always quite understand his fans and why they do the things they do, he remained steadfast in his good feelings.

He said in an interview that appeared on the Reuters Web site that the fan reaction "is pretty hard to comprehend. Everything is just kind of surreal. I have no clue."

Justin may not have a clue but he continued to defend his fans' actions.

"I don't think the fans are too obsessed," he said in a May 9 interview with CNN International. "The fans are really supportive and I'm glad I have really devoted fans. As far as all the stuff that happens, I guess they do what they gotta do."

That particular statement, acknowledging that his fans are beyond his control, would prove prophetic. On May 10, news broke that a water bottle that Justin drank out of during a New Zealand trip was put up for auction on an Internet site and sold for $855.

While all of this appears to be harmless fun and nothing more, those around Justin have been aware for a long time that fans could possibly snap and go to the dark side. Typical of the attention to security surrounding the young singer is the degree to which anything sent to Justin is monitored. In a recent interview with *Time* magazine, Justin said that although he loves to read his fan mail, "I get a lot of candy sent to me but I'm not allowed to eat it because my mom said it might be poisonous."

However the world looks at Justin and his meteoric rise, one thing is certain. Pop culture runs in cycles and inevitably there will be pot shots taken. Early in 2010, E! Online ran an article, complete with quotes from reputable child psychologists, indicating that Justin was on the verge of being out of control himself, and cited examples that he was rapidly turning into a diva at the ripe old age of sixteen.

One example not cited by E! but that added fuel to the "Bieber as Diva" theory emerged in late May when a series of items appeared in the likes of *The Daily Telegraph* and other Australian and UK outlets that indicated a less than cute pop star side to Justin.

According to the reports, on his previous visit to Australia, Justin reportedly dropped a four letter obscenity on a staff member of the morning chat show *Sunrise Seven*. According to the show's co-anchor, David Koch, at one point in the program, "Our floor manager was directing him to the spot where he was to perform and (Bieber) turned around and said to him 'Don't ever **** touch me again.'"

Koch conceded that it had been a hectic day on the show and that everyone was under a tremendous amount of pressure. "Things get said in the heat of the moment and that was just one of those things." He did, however, relate a conversation he had with Justin's sound technician at the time of the incident who indicated that Justin's behavior that day was "regular."

When informed on his "alleged" misbehavior in Australia, Justin immediately went on the defensive, tweeting his fans to the effect that he knew better than to disrespect others. "I was raised to respect others and not gossip," he tweeted. "I know my friends, family and fans know the person I am. Hearing adults spread lies and rumors is part of the job, I guess."

Justin and his team have categorically denied any and all allegations, stating in no uncertain terms that he is well adjusted and comfortable in his situation. Nevertheless, a lot of people tend to forget that Justin is still a teenager and that, while responding with professional ease to the attacks, emotionally the sixteen-year-old must have been taking extreme offense to such charges. In a tweet that was published by Uinterview, Justin exposed a bit of how upset he was. "It's funny when I read things about myself that are just not true. Why would people take time out from their day to hate on a sixteen-year-old?"

Usher, in particular, has stated that Justin was the perfect hero for our time. Braun, while denying the suggestion that Justin was turning into an uncontrollable monster, explained to an Associated Press reporter how he and others are keeping Justin on the straight and narrow. He said that he is constantly showing Justin examples of child stars whose careers and lives have gone wrong so that he can learn from their failures as well as their successes. He cited as a prime example the life of Michael Jackson, who Justin has long admired.

"There's a sense that I need to help him grow up as a man," he said. "I'm going to help him become a good adult. If he's a good man, then he should be able to handle being a celebrity as a man. If the talent's still there, the talent's there."

But as the days began to wind down to the first date on Justin's first headlining tour, he had more pressing things on his agenda than what a bunch of journalists who had run out of angles to write about thought of him, and what kind of picture of him they were trying to paint.

The video for his next single, "Somebody to Love,"

was scheduled to be shot late in May. There was little to report because, in what is often the case in the music business, the concept had not been decided on yet and no costar had been selected (although Justin had a short list that included Megan Fox and nobody else). Of the video, Justin would only say that "it will be cool, fun, and awesome."

However, Justin could not keep his Twitter finger at rest for long and he quickly followed up with a cryptic tweet to his fans regarding the video. "Secret rehearsals. Sick dance crews. A lot of surprises for this one. David Meyers [who directed videos for the likes of Jay-Z and Britney Spears] is directing. It's a lot of work. It's going to be crazy."

He continued to tweet over the course of what would turn out to be long hours of a two-day video shoot. At one point he informed his fans that Usher had stopped by to hang out. In another message he said he was on his way to the set to do the "backpacker scenes." But for the most part, the "Somebody to Love" video remained a closely guarded secret.

Perhaps Justin savored those few days of the shoot more than he would have in the past. It was work but it was an isolated session with a few friends and coworkers, far from the craziness that had become his life. After doing so many videos, it was a situation that he was more than capable of handling in a professional manner. In fact, just about everyone connected with the shoot acknowledged, with no small touch of amusement and respect, just how good Justin was at doing this kind of thing. He had the patience, the drive, and, crucially, the determination well beyond his years, and it showed in the work, which was first-rate on all counts.

Once his tour began, it would be back to the grind. So Justin, knowing quiet days were not going to last long, appeared laid-back and relaxed.

It goes without saying that when you are as famous as Justin, there are never enough hours in the day. Braun and other members of Justin's team knew that, which was why Justin's days were planned out in detail. Nothing was left to chance. From the moment he got up until the moment he went to sleep, his entourage made sure he knew when and where he had to be and how long each stop would last. But even the best laid itinerary had occasional glitches.

Like most celebrities, Justin would occasionally over-extend himself and have to cancel an appearance. Doing so was something that Justin absolutely hated. He always felt that he was letting somebody down when it happened. Sometimes, though, it just could not be helped.

When the video shoot began to run long, Justin had no choice but to back out of a scheduled appearance at the Young Hollywood Awards show. The event was relatively new. Although it would have been fun to mix and mingle with his contemporaries, completing the video was more important.

Justin's no-show—he did offer up a prerecorded acceptance speech when he captured Newcomer of the Year honors—coupled with the appearance of Miley Cyrus and her steady boyfriend Liam Hemsworth, immediately set tongues wagging with speculation that Justin was afraid to meet up with the guy in light of all the "Justin dating Miley" stories that were circulating.

Once again it was another great story that had no basis in reality. In Justin's world, stuff sometimes happened. But he was not going out of his way to avoid Miley or a public confrontation.

Anticipation for the tour was growing to a fever pitch, and rumors surrounding it were running wild on the Internet. It was known that Sean Kingston would be Justin's opening act, and fans were wondering whether the performers would make an appearance in each other's sets. Rumors also flew that Justin might take a night or two off to appear on shows with Taylor Swift, Selena Gomez, and Rihanna, or that other superstars might make surprise appearances at various stops on his tour. For her part, Rihanna was quick to deny that rumor. Yet it did absolutely nothing to stop it from growing.

There was also speculation swirling around the blogosphere that the young singer might schedule some strategic days off mid-tour to sneak into the studio to record some new songs that were already being written, the theory being that what better way to hype a tour than to debut a brand-new song live and have it immediately jump onto radio playlists. Adding to that rumor was the story that Justin already had some previously recorded but un-released songs that he might decide to drop to keep fans excited until his next album—which, in a best-case sce-nario, was at least another year away. That notion sounded good but, apparently, nobody was ready to cop to it.

At least not completely.

In the meantime, Justin, rather than slowing down, was moving nonstop on the promotion trail. He took a quick hop back to Japan, where he found the Bieber Fever of his last visit undiminished. Again he was mobbed at the airport and followed everywhere he went. He went to din-ner at a fancy restaurant and would later tweet that he was served dinner by ninjas. Justin assured everyone who asked that he appreciated the support of his Japanese fans and would do everything in his power to schedule a concert stop there sometime in the future.

Then it was back to the States, where more rumors were afoot. An offhand remark by celebrity TV host Ryan Seacrest floated the possibility that Justin would replace Simon Cowell as a judge on next season's *American Idol*. This story was partially supported by the announcement that Justin would sing on the season finale of the show. From a purely business sense, being an *American Idol* judge would be too much of a strain on his already impossible schedule and the rumor might have been an attempt by the show's producers to boost *American Idol's* flagging ratings.

Justin made good on a May 19 *American Idol* appearance, though. It was a somewhat nostalgic and ironic experience for him. He had achieved what the contestants were trying so hard for and as a youngster had already made his way to the top. But what if the fates had dealt him a different hand? The show is largely a popularity contest, with actual talent often taking a backseat. In such an arena, would Justin have actually won if he had been on the show? And then there was the matter of freedom. Justin had heard the *American Idol* winners were under strict control, basically being told what and how to sing. It's a good bet that if Justin had won *American Idol*, he probably would never have been allowed to bring in Ludacris to help out on a song like "Baby." That would not have been a safe musical choice to sell to Middle America.

That said, however, Justin did have a good time revisiting his childhood fantasies when appearing on the show. And his ego flexed mightily when he was approached by the show's remaining contestants for advice and encouragement. In his own way, Justin demonstrated that he already had *American Idol*–style skills when he performed two of his signature songs, "Baby" and "U Smile," which brought the house down.

From the start, Justin's image had been built upon an image of purity, and in keeping with the Christian values instilled in him by his mother. But while Justin had turned into a bigger-than-life superstar, his very human hormones were also starting to kick in. There had been numerous reports over the past year that Justin was becoming a bit more frisky and flirtatious around his female fans in general and older women in particular.

So more than one person in Justin's team was a bit concerned in May when, while doing promotion on a radio show, Justin gave some surprisingly candid responses to the typical "What's your love life like?" questions posed by the radio hosts.

He was quick to admit that he's "a very good kisser," as he put it, a remark reported just about everywhere, including *Access Hollywood*. The comment was in response to how many girls he had made out with. He was vague about the exact number but, when pressed by the radio jocks, he admitted to "a couple of chicks." And while he had yet to kiss a girl in his new Range Rover, he offered that he had a plan for how that might happen. "If you're driving and you make a little stop at the rest stop in Walmart, you're good."

Responses to these remarks were all over the place. Some girls most likely took them as confirmation that their dreams of being Justin's one-and-only were dashed. Others probably saw it as an invitation to try and get close to him, as he had more or less advertised his availability. At the end of the day, it was just Justin being Justin, which translated into being honest regardless of the repercussions.

Personal anecdotes aside, nobody could doubt Justin's power as a singer whose songs remained a constant on radio airwaves and whose ability to sell his music was even bigger than the ups and downs of the record business. This fact was brought up primarily in the trades and business sections in late May when stories began appearing that indicated that, despite an overall downturn in albums sales, *My World 2.0* had just moved back into the number-1 spot on the *Billboard* Pop Chart. It was a fact that set tongues wagging among music industry pundits. But the bottom line was, quite simply, that Justin just had that something.

Which was why every record company and manager was beating the bushes for the next Justin Bieber.

Justin's June 4 return to *The Today Show*'s Summer Concert Series was something the young singer was certainly looking forward to. He was part of an all-star schedule that included performers from Sting to Lady Gaga. His previous appearance on the show, in the eyes of many, had been what broke him out of the teeny bop world into mainstream media. New York City was looking forward to Justin's return as well. And this time they felt they were prepared.

In anticipation of the throngs of young fans who were already making plans to descend on the city, police presence was increased and security measures tightened. Strict regulations about when fans could actually come to Rockefeller Center were laid down. City officials knew that people were going to show up early despite their efforts, so they prepared to deal with that reality in the best way possible.

How New York was reacting to Justin's upcoming appearance was indicative of how security around the world had gotten wise to the news that Justin Bieber was coming to town. History had taught them what an appearance by Justin could result in. Consequently, more stringent efforts were put in place to insure that Justin's fans got close but not too close, and that those fans would go home with happy memories rather than broken bones and emotional trauma. It was the pop star game and everybody had to learn how to play it.

Such preparations made his life a little bit easier. He had noticed it during recent trips to places like Japan. There was still the hysteria and the mobs of screaming girls, but the intensity didn't veer out of control. As such, more interaction with his fans was possible, which was what Justin wanted more than anything else. It was also a sign of respect that Justin could be appreciated but not overwhelmed.

Justin was beside himself with excitement as the days counted down to *The Today Show* appearance. He was already mentally preparing for the upcoming U.S. tour, and this appearance would help him get into that touring mindset and give him a chance to practice his singing and choreography before a live and very large audience, something that no amount of rehearsal time could give him.

There was electricity in the air the morning of June 4.

Frantic teen fans had been crushing the barricades of the Rockefeller Plaza for hours. The screams grew to near the threshold of pain when Justin emerged and launched into a set of his greatest hits. Despite the relatively closed-in area Justin was moving smoothly and like a seasoned pro. His vocals, despite all the mystery of how he would sound now that his voice was changing, were first-rate and soulful. The band and dancers were in tip-top shape. The consensus was that, if anything, Justin's overall professional demeanor had grown more polished and mature than ever before.

As good as the production values had always been on his albums and singles, *The Today Show* appearance was a perfect example of the power of Justin in a live setting. Yes, the polish and silky smooth delivery was very much there. But listening to Justin knock out the likes of "One Time," "One Less Lonely Girl," and "Baby" in the slightly extemporaneous way of all live performances, was to see the essence of what made Justin tick. It made seasoned listeners of his music appreciate the twists and turns he had added to freshen up older material and added to their dreams of what future music might bring.

The crowd surged forward in response to the performance. New York's finest had a bemused look on their faces as they stood between this pint-sized singer and the hordes of screaming teen girls who were doing everything in their power to get to him. It looked like some things would never change.

As he performed, Justin most likely looked upon the adulation of the screaming crowd with no small sense of wonder. He sensed that what he and, for that matter, any teen idol was giving his fans was a fantasy object of desire, dreams, and adulation. His reality was to give millions of fans a fantasy. It was a tough job but one that he was more than willing to do.

Justin was all smiles and visibly excited as he left *The Today Show* stage. You could see it in his eyes as he rushed through the adoring crowd behind a wall of security into his van and was driven away down the streets of New York with the screams of his fans still ringing in his ears.

He could not wait for the tour to start.

19. AND SO IT ENDS

By all accounts, Justin seemed in a good place physically and emotionally. He must have been reminded about the toll a months-long tour could take, and that he should get himself together. Headlining appearances could typically run close to two hours in length. It went without saying that Justin's show would be a high-energy, physically draining performance. Then there was the monotony of interminable plane rides, countless hotels, and more people to deal with than he had ever dealt with before. True, the adrenaline would keep him going at the beginning, but many were speculating what impact the tour would have on Justin two months in.

Justin was told in detail what to expect in the coming months and he most likely took that advice to heart.

The opinion was that he looked as though he was getting more sleep then he had in the past. His school year officially over for the summer gave him three hours a day he could now use to rest and relax. He had often admitted in the past that much of what had gone on in the past three years had been an exciting blur. But he had, by this time, grown to be comfortable with the craziness and to ride with the surprises and unexpected moments that were now a near daily occurrence.

These were all signs that Justin had matured into the role of superstar and the responsibility that goes with it in an amazingly short time, and that he was more than capable of handling his career over the long haul.

Justin and his people were smart enough to not jump immediately into a full-blown, headlining concert tour without a bit of warm-up. Consequently, Justin ramped up to the tour and his arrival in Hartford with a couple of mighty big "rehearsal" events.

May 14 saw him participating in a mega show in Chula Vista, California, the Summer Concert Kickoff show sponsored by radio station 93.3 in San Diego. The all-star lineup included Usher, Ke$ha, Akon, and Iyaz. It was the kind of concert tailor-made for the summer, a long show with lots of acts and a good-time feel. In other words, one big party.

For Justin, the prospect of appearing on the same bill as Usher and to see firsthand how he works a large crowd was an education he could not have obtained elsewhere.

And the look on Usher's face as he watched Justin take over the spotlight was an emotional moment for both mentor and protégé.

The Chula Vista show was very close to what his tour set would be like, apart from some slight modifications for the show's running time and lighting. According to those who observed it, he had come through with flying colors.

The May 15 Wango Tango concert in Los Angeles had also served as a good preparation for the tour. The scope of the all-star concert, which has been an annual event in Los Angeles for a number of years, allowed Justin to roll out the full complement of musicians and dancers. It had featured a hint of the lighting effects he would use to full effect on his tour, and the size of the stage had facilitated his choreography and timing. When it came to performing in front of an audience of thousands, Justin had long since gotten that down, as the packed house cheered his every move and every song.

The set consisted of seven songs, all the hits and then some. However, what really stood out in the performance was the more divergent nature of the interplay between Justin and the band. Justin's generous attitude allowed for each band member to solo at points in the show before settling back into their support groove. It was a sign of respect between singer and band that showcased Justin as wise and savvy beyond his years.

It was a hell of a warm-up. Hartford would be the main event.

But before that happened Justin's tattoo again became the topic of conversation. It had already been reported in March that Justin had continued a family tradition by having a small bird tattooed on his hip, inspired by the novel *Jonathan Livingston Seagull*. It was forgotten by the press until May 18, when pictures of Justin in a Toronto tattoo parlor being tattooed under the watchful eye of his proud father, Jeremy, hit the Internet.

MTV recently interviewed the tattoo shop's co-owner Brian Byrne, who explained that Justin's tattoo was done shortly after his sixteenth birthday as a birthday present. "When Justin, his father, Jeremy, and the tattoo artist, a family friend named Charlie, came down, we were asked if we could keep it quiet. So we made sure that the shop was empty and that there was nobody around."

The tattoo was to be positioned on Justin's left hip, which, explained Byrne, can be an extremely painful area. Justin got through the experience without a whimper. "He was nervous at first but then he got into it. He laid there and sucked it up. His dad took a bunch of pictures and video and everybody talked to him while it was being done. Pretty soon it was done. He's a very nice kid and we'd be happy to have him back if he ever wanted any more work."

There was much speculation about Justin's tattoo, with

some conservative hand wringers concerned about how the tattoo would impact his life and career. But for die-hard fans, the only response was how cool it was. Like most Justin news, the story was hot for a couple of days . . . until the next report of what Justin was up to hit the internet.

Justin remained a fairly normal, level-headed kid. However, he could not be blamed if after three years of such adulation, he had become a bit jaded. Perhaps because he was still so young, the process and the experience remained exciting. Needles to say, that was a good thing.

The reality was that, despite barely topping out at five foot five, he had truly cast a giant shadow in terms of ushering in a different way of doing music business, one that would most likely be copied in the years to come.

Justin did not invent the Internet and the idea of music videos as a way of promoting his songs. We have the advent of MTV to thank for that. However, the whole process had evolved from the days of Duran Duran and VJ's. The way Justin had used the medium was definitely the next step forward.

It went without saying that using the Internet to find and cultivate a loyal fan base was the key to Justin's success. And rather than spending years paying his dues in small clubs, going the prefab Disney/Nickelodeon route to stardom, or relying on such shows as *American Idol* for his big break, Justin was discovered through the posting of raw performance videos and reaching out to millions of online friends, who would find and pass his talents on down the information highway.

There were already those picking up on Justin's blue-print for success and running with it. Josh Perry, a sixteen-year-old who recently captured honors on the UK television show *Britain's Got Talent*, has already been hearing the Justin Bieber comparisons, which he is taking great pains to deny while, at the same time, paying his proper respects. And in the States, a twelve-year-old named Jordan Jansen, who has been posting his performance videos for four years as a gift to his grandmother, recently went to Los Angeles to record his first album.

An Edmond, Oklahoma, twelve-year-old named Greyson Chance, looking very much like Justin, amazed his schoolmates and teachers during a school music festival when he sat down at the piano and sang a perfect rendition of Lady Gaga's song "Paparazzi." On the surface, it may have all been nothing more innocent than taping the performance. But perhaps there was an ulterior motive at work here because Greyson's performance was taped and subsequently put up on YouTube, where it would attract 8 million viewers. Ellen DeGeneres heard about this new Internet hero and, in an attempt to get the jump on the next Justin Bieber, arranged for the young boy to appear on her show. During his appearance, Lady Gaga called in to congratulate and encourage the youngster.

Not surprisingly there would be others, as kids all over the world suddenly saw stars in their eyes. When he heard about the Greyson song, Justin most likely was outwardly polite and encouraging, though he was probably having a quiet laugh at this form of flattery.

At least until the Twitter site changed its formula for calculating the most popular topics, which, amazingly, resulted in Justin dropping out of the Twitter top ten and Greyson Chance suddenly appearing. Whether it was jealousy or a sudden bit of insecurity, Justin immediately tweeted the company, wanting to know what was going on. Almost immediately he again appeared in Twitter's top ten. Yes, at sixteen years old Justin definitely had the power to change people's minds. Of course it did not hurt that Justin's millions of fans had immediately jumped to the young singer's defense when they began bombarding Twitter central with tweets of protest.

It was about the time when all the supposed pretenders to the Justin Bieber throne were making their presence known that Justin received the greatest compliment a singer could get. In the space of two weeks, two other talented teen singers, Charice, who had appeared on *The Oprah Winfrey Show* with Justin, and Kinna Grannis, both announced that they had covered his song "Baby" for their upcoming albums.

Adding still more icing to the Justin Bieber cake was a late-May announcement that the singer had received a Best New Artist nomination from the prestigious BET Awards Show. Any nomination is good but what made the BET nod so gratifying is that Justin was being included in a ceremony that normally honors only black performers. Stephen Hill, BET's president of music and specials, told a Reuters reporter why Justin was an exception to the rule: "Bieber has crossed the color boundaries the same way that hip-hop has crossed boundaries the other way. He has rhythm in his music. He makes the kind of music that our audience likes."

P. Diddy and other black artists would also come forward in defending the nomination, saying in essence that good music should be color-blind.

Until now, Justin had seemed indifferent to what most people might perceive as competition. But that feeling may well have struck a different chord when, mere days after his appearance on *The Ellen DeGeneres Show,* Greyson Chance was signed to a recording contract with Interscope Records, which, coincidentally, is Lady Gaga's label. Not long after that announcement, Greyson used Justin's Twitter ploy to let people know that he was working on some new songs and that he was getting ready to record.

While industry critics were not too surprised and had predicted that others would copy the Justin Bieber blueprint for success, it was also soon being speculated that the trend of Internet videos leading to worldwide audiences and recording deals could very well put a dent in the importance of talent shows like *American Idol* and other more traditional forms of dues paying as a pathway to stardom. Taken to the extreme end, it could push aside truly individual, creative musicians and music in favor of a tidal wave of preteen Justin Bieber clones.

Only time would tell.

Greyson soon found himself in the middle of a Justin-style frenzy of media speculation and interest. The young newcomer was immediately the subject of Internet gossip. Not surprisingly, he was compared to Justin, and those looking to stir up controversy were so bold as to suggest that Greyson actually had more talent than Justin. Greyson, who also used Twitter as his communication tool of choice, indicated in a tweet that was picked up by Softpedia that it was an honor to be compared to Justin and that he hoped to one day go on tour with him.

Justin appreciated the compliment but was too busy working on his own music to respond to the notion of helping somebody else. It was most certainly nothing personal against Greyson Chance. It was just business.

As the countdown to Justin's tour continued, it was widely speculated that Justin's management team, in particular Braun, was in behind-the-scenes meetings with several major film and television studio producers to discuss the possibility of making Justin's desire to act a reality. There were continued talks about a Justin biopic, sort of a teen-friendly version of the movie *8 Mile*. Braun seemed equally intent on developing a television series for Justin and, according to Entertainment Daily, was in active discussion with screenwriters and producers on developing a starring role for Justin.

How successful those negotiations were became a reality on May 19 when the story hit Acesshowbiz and numerous other outlets that Warner Bros. had slotted Justin on a short list of actors to be in the sequel to the movie *Valentine's Day*, entitled *New Year's Eve*. This came as news to director Garry Marshall, who had already been tapped to direct the sequel.

"I hear that they [Warner Bros.] keep mentioning this Justin Bieber," he said. "I have no idea who he is. Perhaps I'd better see who he is so when he arrives on the set, we can talk."

The timing for Justin to do the movie would be perfect. His tour would be winding down around the time of the September 2010 start of production on *New Year's Eve*. Even better, it would be filmed in New York, which would likely put Justin just a stone's throw away from the recording studio.

Justin had always been earnest in his desire to act. But in a Reuters interview conducted around the time of the movie announcement, he could not help but have a little fun with the prospect. "In ten years you'll see me in *Ocean's 60* or something," he said with a chuckle. "It'll be a Bieber–Brad Pitt matchup but he'll be, like, 180 by then."

Justin in the space of three years had defied the odds, been more than a bit lucky, and had proved that anything is possible—and there was a legion of young people who were eager to follow in his footsteps. Success was changing everything. Even the things he felt certain he wanted to do.

It was a pretty good guess that his supposed plans to go to a public high school in the fall had fallen by the wayside. He would be in the middle of his tour around the time the bell rang for first period. And as soon as the tour ended, there would be more songs to record, albums to release; maybe a movie or two. No, private on-the-road tutors would be the way he would go as long as he continued his education.

The only thing anyone knew for certain was that the career of Justin Bieber was now in full swing and, for better or worse, he would never be a normal kid again. But that didn't mean Justin would give up his adolescence without a fight.

In a recent interview with the *Sun* he stated that he would continue his high school education until he was eighteen and then would very seriously consider going to college. "I don't want to limit my options," he said. "You never know how things are going to turn out. And I want to be ready for anything."

As Justin gets ready to step out on his first national headlining tour, one thing is certain: Justin Bieber's time is now.

Epilogue
WHAT HAPPENS
IN STRATFORD

To set the record straight, Justin Bieber is not the first big-time celebrity to come out of Stratford, Ontario. Lloyd Robertson, a well-known broadcaster, is famous in these parts. And two-time Stanley Cup hockey champion Tim Taylor is not chopped liver. The actor Colm Feore. Opera singers James Westman and Roger Honeywell. Well, you get the picture.

So how has Stratford responded to a favorite son becoming the biggest thing since Elvis and the Beatles? They've quite literally put Justin on the map. Beginning in May 2010, and reported amid a boatload of journalism by the *Toronto Star's* Ashante Infantry, the city has added a Justin-flavored element to its tourist Web site in which a downloadable map indicates places where Justin hung out, the schools he attended, his favorite restaurants—just about everything a pop-music historian would want to know.

As Stratford is a relatively small town, almost everybody knew somebody who knew somebody who knew Justin. In an article published in the *Toronto Star*, people were tracked down who knew him then and now. Norma Henderson said her granddaughter attended kindergarten with him. Alecia Kyle claimed to know his cousin. Reportedly he had family in the nearby hamlet of Mitchell, and would spend a lot of the time there.

So that was then. What about now?

It is known that Justin has made several trips back to Stratford since hitting the big time, usually for just a day or two to see family and friends. On a recent visit, mayor Dan Mathieson told the *Star* that Justin wanted to pay a visit to one of his old haunts, the YMCA. A $4 admission charge was required for a day visit. Mathieson offered to have the city waive the fee but Justin responded, "That's okay, I have a credit card when I travel."

Still, the town is ambivalent about Justin's success. On the one hand, they are extremely proud of him, but they are careful to avoid coming across as exploiting him for the sake of tourism. An attempt has been made to have a Justin Bieber Day celebration in the town but, at the moment, Justin's extremely busy schedule has kept them from establishing such an event.

However, Justin definitely put Stratford on the map.

While the fan mania surrounding him has not reached the proportion of the Stephenie Meyer craze in Forks, Washington, there is the occasional trickle of giggly girls, prowling the streets and looking for the places where Justin used to hang out. Some Justin-related merchandise is available in area stores, and it's a foregone conclusion that anybody looking for a Justin CD (yes, there are a few people on the planet that don't have them) or a good story about what a very young Justin Bieber was like, could find what they're looking for in Long & McQuade's Music Store.

And there are the fan letters. Although Justin now calls Atlanta his home, letters regularly arrive at Stratford addressed simply "Justin Bieber, Stratford, Ontario, Canada." With no way of forwarding the mail, the Stratford Post Office has done what any small-town post office would do.

The letters all go to Justin's grandmother.

DISCOGRAPHY

THE ALBUMS

My World

SONGS: "One Time," "Favorite Girl," "Down to Earth," "Bigger," "One Less Lonely Girl," "First Dance," "Love Me"

HIGHEST CHART POSITION:
Number 5 on *Billboard* Top 200
Number 79 in Australia
Number 18 in Austria
Number 16 in Belgium
Number 1 in Canada
Number 18 in Germany
Number 10 in Greece

Number 11 in Ireland
Number 22 in Mexico
Number 19 in Poland
Number 39 in Sweden
Number 4 in the United Kingdom

My World 2.0

SONGS: "Baby," "Somebody to Love," "Stuck in the Moment," "U Smile," "Runaway Love," "Never Let You Go," "Overboard," "Eenie Meenie," "Up," "That Should Be Me," "Kiss and Tell," "Where Are You Now"

HIGHEST CHART POSITION:
Number 1 on *Billboard* Top 200
Number 2 in Austria
Number 1 in Australia
Number 3 in Belgium
Number 1 in Brazil
Number 1 in Canada
Number 30 in the Czech Republic
Number 13 in Finland
Number 4 in France
Number 7 in Germany
Number 4 in Greece
Number 1 in Ireland
Number 14 in Italy
Number 2 in Mexico
Number 1 in New Zealand

Number 3 in Norway
Number 22 in Poland
Number 2 in Portugal
Number 6 in Spain
Number 2 in Sweden
Number 21 in Switzerland
Number 3 in the United Kingdom

THE SINGLES

"One Time"

HIGHEST CHART POSITION:
Number 17 on *Billboard* Hot 100, Number 14 on *Billboard*
Pop Songs

"One Less Lonely Girl"

HIGHEST CHART POSITION:
Number 16 on *Billboard* Hot 100

"Love Me"

HIGHEST CHART POSITION:
Number 37 on *Billboard* Hot 100

"Favorite Girl"

HIGHEST CHART POSITION:
Number 26 on *Billboard* Hot 100

"Baby"

HIGHEST CHART POSITION:
Number 5 on *Billboard* Hot 100

"Never Let You Go"

HIGHEST CHART POSITION:
Number 21 on *Billboard* Hot 100

"U Smile"

HIGHEST CHART POSITION:
Number 27 on *Billboard* Hot 100

"Somebody to Love"

HIGHEST CHART POSITION:
Number 35 on Mainstream Top 40 (National Top 40 Singles Chart)

"Eenie Meenie"

HIGHEST CHART POSITION:
Number 15 on *Billboard* Hot 100

Memorable Song Performances

"One Time"

The song was the last number of Justin's set during his two
nights of opening for Taylor Swift in the UK.

He was right in the middle of singing that song on the first
night when he fractured his foot.

He performed the song on *Dick Clark's New Year's Rockin'
Eve* show.

Justin did an acoustic version of the song with an added
drum solo on the Blue Water BBC show.

"One Less Lonely Girl"

Justin performed an acoustic version of the song for the first
time on the Canadian TV show *The Next Star*.

The song was part of his set on his US network TV debut,
on *The Today Show*.

During his performance of the song during Z100's Jingle
Ball concert, he called good friend Caitlin Beadles on
stage and sang to her.

Justin's performance of the song on the Help for Haiti telethon was highlighted by his singing the first verse of the
song in French.

"Love Me"

Justin performed the song in an unaired segment of VH1's *Pepsi Super Bowl Fan Jam.* The segment would subsequently be made available on the Internet.

The song was considered a high point in Justin's 2010 appearance at the Houston rodeo, a concert bill he shared with Selena Gomez.

"Favorite Girl"

Justin performed the song acoustically for the first time on *The Ellen DeGeneres Show.*

During a live MTV Artist of the Week session, he performed the song while playing a keyboard.

"Baby"

The first acoustic version of the song was performed on *MuchMusic.*

Justin performed the song for the first time with Ludacris on the Help for Haiti telethon. During this performance he changed the lyrics in the chorus to "baby, baby, Haiti" to show support for the cause.

Justin performed the song with Drake on the 2010 Juno Awards.

"Never Let You Go"

Justin performed the song at the grand opening of the Microsoft Store in Mission Viejo, California.

He sang the song on the TV program *The Early Show* as part
of their Super Bowl programming.

"U Smile"

Justin performed the song during his appearance on *Saturday
Night Live*.

A SHORT LIST OF TEEN IDOLS (1980-2010)

There have been teen idols since the 1900s. Good-looking boys and girls who acted or sang their way into young girls' and boys' hearts and imaginations. Since the odds are pretty high that most of you would not remember anybody who was around pre-1980, that year seemed like a good choice to start the list of pioneers who helped pave the way for Justin Bieber. So, in no particular order . . .

"The Guys"

Michael Jackson, New Kids on the Block, Backstreet Boys, *NSync, Jonas Brothers, New Edition, Menudo, Boyz II Men, Marky Mark, Kris Kross, Immature, Hanson, Aaron Carter, Lil Bow Wow, O Town, Chris Brown.

"The Girls"

Britney Spears, Miley Cyrus, Christina Aguilera, Debbie Gibson, Tiffany, Brandy, Rihanna, Taylor Swift, Selena Gomez.

sources

Quite simply, the media has done its job. The press has examined the Justin Bieber story from every conceivable angle and has made researching this book an entertaining and enlightening experience. Many thanks to all the reporters, interviewers, and journalists for a job well done.

The Associated Press and many magazines and newspapers contributed to the cause. They include: *The New York Times, Toronto Star, Entertainment Weekly, Billboard, Rolling Stone, Ottawa Citizen, Maclean's Magazine, London Observer, Los Angeles Times, Teen Daily, StarShine Magazine, J-14, Tiger Beat, Bop, Houston Chronicle, Teen Vogue, London Daily, London Daily Telegraph, USA Today, New Zealand Herald, Calgary Sun, Twist, Philadelphia Daily News, Details, Interview, Def Jam Press Release, The Boston Globe, The Washington Post, BBC Music, People,*

US, M Magazine, Star, Toronto Sun, First News, Time, New York Post, Reuters News Service, Life & Style Magazine, The Republic.

As always, hats off to the Web sites, fan pages, and news sites for their hard work and diligence. They include: Ace Showbiz.com, MTV, Wikipedia, Billboard.com, Stratford Ontario, Canada.com, RapidDiscoveryMedia.com, Miss O & Friends.com, NewYorkTimes.com, VH1.com, World Press.com, DisneyDreaming.com, Oceanup.com, TheStar .com, Justinbiebermusic.com, LATimes.com, JustinBieber Tour.net, EW.com, Starpulse.com, Showbizspy.com, Examiner.com, Complex.com, Crushable.com, CTVW5.com, BET .com, DigitalSpy.com, Splashnews.com, Dailyfill.com, Bitten andBound.com, JustJaredJr.com, JSYK.com, Neon Limelight .com, IntheKnow.com, Popstar.com, GMTV.com, ABC-News.com, TopofthePops.com, WWWQ Radio, Squiddo .com, CNN, YoungHollywood.com, National Examiner.com, About.com, Canadaeast.com, AccessHollywood.com, AOL .com, KansasCity.com, TheGuardian.co.uk, Softpedia, GameOn.com, Entertainment Daily, WENN, NewsTimes .com, Popdirt.com.